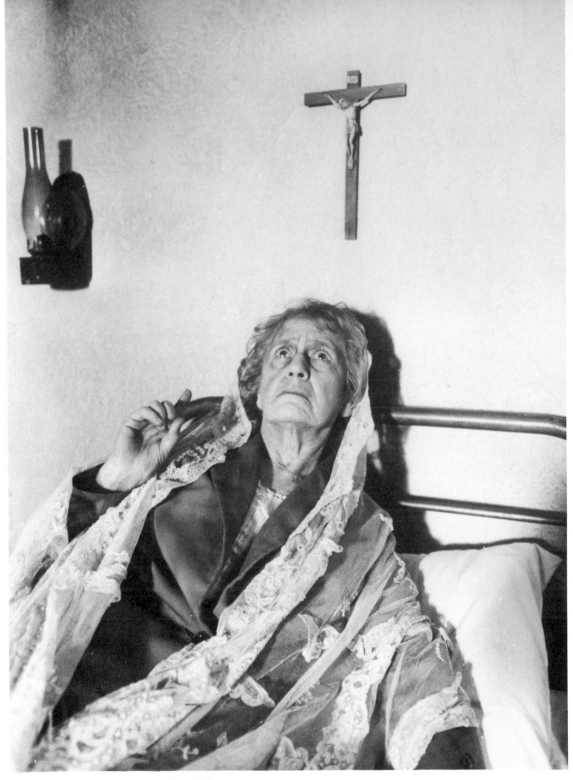

Frontispiece   Dame Peggy Ashcroft in a scene from the film *The Jewel in the Crown*, wearing the first veil made by the author. (*Photograph courtesy of Granda TV [Manchester]*)

Nenia Lovesey

Larousse & Co., Inc. New York

ACKNOWLEDGMENT

My thanks to Dot Humphry, Mary Harbard and Maureen Lovesey for the endless reading, correcting and typing of the text for the third time around; I can honestly say we are still friends. Thanks also to the girls who have spent hours over the work they have produced for the photographs, notably Catherine Barley, Doreen Holmes, Pat Gibson, Ann Forbes-Cockell, Mary Anderson, Shirley, Janie, Elsa, Vera and my two students from Portsmouth, Hampshire, who will always be known as Supersonic and Jetlag. I am indebted to Granada Television Limited, Manchester, for allowing me to use two stills from the television series *The Jewel in the Crown*. I should also like to thank Peter Harris who was responsible for the rest of the photography, Mr Hall for the research he has carried out for the afficots and Sadie Vaughan for checking the typescript. Lastly but not least, my especial thanks go to my husband, who has calmly taken everything in his stride and has given me endless help and encouragement.

ISBN 0–88332–443–1
LCCN 84–082383

First published in USA 1985 by
Larousse & Co., Inc.
572 Fifth Avenue
New York, N.Y. 10036

Printed in Great Britain

Contents

Glossary   7

Introduction   8

1   Background to Needlepoint Lace   11
2   Materials and Preparation   22
3   The Stitches   27
4   Raised Work   48
5   Designing   55
6   Edgings and Patterns   67
7   Poupée and Pandore   94
Conclusion   108

Suppliers   117
Index   119

The first veil was lost when the warehouse holding all the props for the film was gutted by fire. With the help of Joan Merrifield from Billericay who worked all the tambour flounce, the author was able to work the needlepoint lace butterflies and flower design that forms the basis of the veil. It is being held here by Geraldine James, accompanied by Nicholas le Prevost. (*Photograph courtesy of Granada TV [Manchester]*)

GLOSSARY

Afficot An instrument used for polishing the raised parts of the lace. Early afficots were made from highly polished wood, bone or ivory, in the shape of a miniature golf club. On the Continent, and later in this country, a lobster claw was cleaned and polished and set into a wooden handle; this was common practice amongst the poorer lacemakers.

Bars or brides The connecting threads across spaces joining one motif or design to another.

Buttonhole stitch Often referred to in the old history and pattern books as close stitch; the basic stitch of needlepoint lace that, in its many variations, forms the grounds, filings and couronnes.

Casket A space in the background entirely surrounded by the design.

Cordonnet The foundation threads that hold the working stitches.

Cordonnette A thick thread or threads laid round the main outline of the design and worked over in close buttonhole stitch; in some laces thick thread is overcast separately and attached to the outline after the lace is finished.

Couching Laying the cordonnet threads round the design and attaching them to the background material with small, evenly spaced stitches.

Couronnes The decoration of the cordonnette, used mainly in Venetian Point and giving the finished lace the look of carved ivory.

Ell In 1101 a law was passed in England stating that an ell should measure 114 cm (45 in) while a Flemish ell was only 68 cm (27 in). Overseers would mark the lace at the beginning, and every ell would then be marked, usually with a little rounded tag. The workers were paid by the ell.

Engrêlure Narrow, bobbin-made edge worked on to needlepoint lace and attached to garment with running stitch for easy removal.

Ground Background pattern, either formed of bars or a mesh, that supports the design motifs.

La trace Alternative method of working a cordonnette.

Mezzo Punto Seventeenth-century, Venetian tape lace.

Pandore Small version of poupée.

Picot A small loop used to enrich an outline of a motif and also to decorate bars, etc.

Pillow Used to support work when working with very fine threads, leaving both hands free to manipulate the threads into position.

Pin stitch Neat, strong method of joining or inserting lace to material.

Point Plat A lace made without a cordonnette so there were no raised parts.

Poupée Fashion doll, over 76 cm (2 ft 6 in) high, popular during the reign of Louis XIV and later.

Purls Type of picot.

Raised work Achieved by buttonholing the cordonnette to give the work a sculptured appearance, or by adding separate, oversewn rings to the finished work.

Réseau Background mesh used to hold together designs not heavy enough to be held together by bars alone.

Ring stick Stick with graduated proportions along its length, used to make couronnes.

Tape lace Mixed lace; bobbin-made braid with needlepoint fillings, originating in the seventeenth-century – probably in Naples.

Toile A mesh or ground.

Veins A row of small holes, interspersed in corded or close Bruxelles stitch, used in Venetian leaves.

Introduction

It is inevitable that sections of this book will overlap information given in *The Technique of Needlepoint Lace* and the *Creative Designs in Needlepoint Lace* that followed. The object of writing this present volume is to gather together all the necessary instructions to give the reader the knowledge to work needlepoint lace without having to jump from one book to the other. There are snippets of history dispersed throughout this book, but students of the City and Guilds textiles examinations should turn to *The Technique of Needlepoint Lace*. Embroiderers use many of the needlepoint lace stitches, using a background material to work the stitches into, for techniques such as cutwork, reticella, richelieu and stumpwork, and students sitting the City and Guilds embroidery examinations will find an affinity with the *Creative Design in Needlepoint Lace*.

This book is an introduction to a long-lost art form, very beautiful to look at and very enjoyable to work, and it is very rewarding to be able to wear something that would cost so much to buy. John Ruskin (1819–1900), the art critic of the nineteenth century, sent a letter to the Duke of St Albans, from which the following has been taken:

> A spider may perhaps be rationally proud of his own cobweb, even though all the fields in the morning are covered with the like, for he made it himself.
>
> But suppose a machine spun it for him? Suppose all the gossamer were Nottingham made? If you think of it, you will find the whole value of lace as a possession depends on the fact of it having a beauty which has been the reward of industry and attention. That the thing is itself a price – a thing everybody cannot have; that it proves, by the look of it, the ability of the maker; that it proves, by the rarity of it, the dignity of its wearer – either that she has been so industrious as to save money, which can buy, say a piece of jewellery, of gold tissue or of fine lace – or else that she is a noble person, to whom her neighbours concede as an honour the priviledge of wearing finer dress than they. If they all choose to have lace too – if it ceases to be a price, it becomes, does it not, only a cobweb.
>
> The real good of a piece of lace then, you will find, is that it should show first that the designer of it had a pretty fancy; next that the maker of it had fine fingers; lastly that the wearer of it has the worthiness or dignity enough to obtain what it is difficult to obtain, and the common sense enough not to wear it on all occasions.

That was written in 1873 and the sentiments still hold good today.

There are two distinct types of hand-made lace; one is made with bobbins worked on a hard pillow, the other is needle-made lace. The width of bobbin lace is dependent on as many bobbins as there are threads, and relies on the bobbin to manipulate the thread through many dexterous moves to form the pattern. Threads are woven one over and under the other to form the solid parts of the pattern and are separated by twisting pairs of threads together to leave gaps or holes. Together these form the design. Needlepoint lace is worked with one thread forming a series of loops. When the loops are placed close together it forms the equivalent of the solid parts of bobbin lace. When spaced at regular intervals it forms the gaps or holes of

Two pieces worked by Elsa Took during her first needlepoint lace classes

8

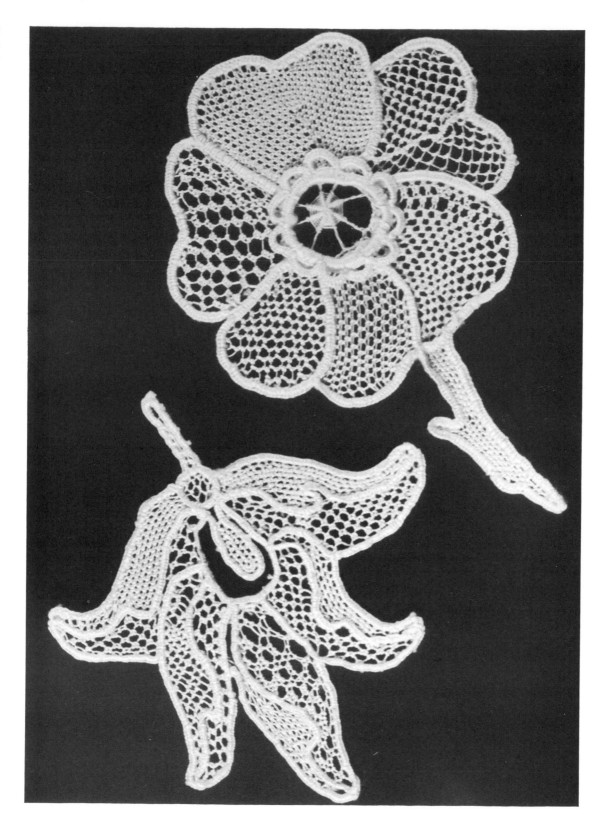

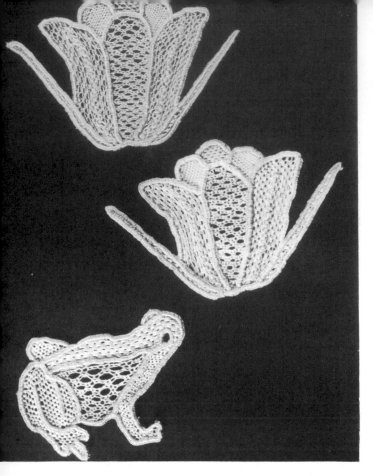

Two flowers by Christine Potbury and a frog by Anne Smith

the design. Some very early needle-made lace can be confusing, because the pattern is held together by needle-weaving, which forms bars looking identical to the bars made with four bobbins forming a plait; the pattern itself, however, will be looped in the needle-made version.

Needlepoint lace was in existence long before bobbin lace and, as early as the Renaissance period, embroidery in the form of cutwork and pulled work – i.e. with the threads of the fabric cut away or pulled aside – had almost arrived at the stage where it was closer to lace than it was to embroidery. The first pattern books of this reticella lace started to circulate among the ladies of the French Court in the latter half of the sixteenth century and the first, and most generally acknowledged, was written by the Venetian, Federico Vinciolo. There are many editions of this book, the first dating from 1597, but it is still avail-

able today as a paperback facsimile. It does include network and lacis, the name given to darned net, but there were some very fine motifs that could not really be classed as cutwork. There were the warp and the weft threads connecting one motif to another, but the geometric patterns were giving way to curves which meant that the thread had to be couched down round them, and the basic threads of the warp and weft were no longer a part of the design.

The new embroidery was termed *Punto in Aria,* or 'stitches in the air'. Reticella borders were given Punto in Aria edgings. Portraits of the Princess of Mantua and Queen Elizabeth I, painted around 1600, show the Vandyke Points of this new type of embroidery. The introduction of Punto in Aria marked a considerable development in the uses to which this new lace could be applied. Now, nearly four centuries later, there is a resurgence of interest in needle-point lace, and the way it is now being worked and the new uses being found for it would have intrigued our forebears.

There are many different types of lace worked with a needle. These instructions will cover a number of them, but not any one in particular. Having mastered the stitches and working methods, going on to a favourite type of lace will be a simple progression.

1. Background to Needlepoint Lace

General method of working

The development of *Punto in Aria* meant that the worker was no longer dependent on the material background and could be much freer with the design. A pattern with the design stamped on to it was attached to another strong piece of linen. A foundation thread – the cordonnet – was laid round the outline of the design and was couched down to both layers. The fillings were then worked into the design spaces. The motifs were joined together with bars, which were made up of buttonhole stitches, and later, as the bars became very costly and time-consuming to produce, the pattern was held together by meshwork, or réseau, which was rows of open-work buttonhole stitches. Once all the design and background were finished, if the design was to be raised, a cordonnette was worked by buttonholing or oversewing the cordonnet to give a slightly raised outline. Parts of the cordonnette were padded with double or treble threads and then oversewn or buttonholed, and the edges were decorated with tiny loops and picots, often very intricate. At other times, couronnes were worked separately in the form of rings which were padded, oversewn and decorated with picots and then applied to the lace. Lastly, the stitches holding the cordonnet were cut between the pattern and the background material and the piece of lace was lifted off.

Not all laces were raised. If the solid parts of the design were worked level and without an outline, it was known as flatwork or Flat Point. In these cases a narrow band of Bruxelles (buttonhole) stitch was worked around the motif to give a sharp defined edge, and the fillings were worked within the shape; if the fillings were worked straight from the cordonnet the rows were inclined to slip. This type of lace always had a mesh background as the edges of the motifs would have been too pliable to keep their shape if bars had been attached. Flat lace had neither a right nor wrong side, but the raised lace did, and was worked with the right side uppermost.

An infinite variety of designs were produced in Venice in the sixteenth and seventeenth centuries, and interest spread all over Europe. It is worth giving here a short description of the characteristics of the different types of lace;

A point de Venise collar owned by Catherine Barley; the front view showing the lappets

The back view of the Venetian collar, showing the typical Point de Venise edge

for a full history and description, see *The Techniques of Needlepoint Lace*. Although certain stitches were associated with certain types of lace, the fillings gradually became universally used in Europe, and it was the background meshes and bars that distinguished one type from another.

RAISED LACES

Venetian Gros Point

This lace was made from the mid-sixteenth century and can be distinguished by the boldness and continuity of the designs. The raised work was the main feature, edged with scallops and with many added couronnes and picots. The motifs were connected by irregular bars, but these did not form part of the pattern; they were purely to hold together the very solid motifs at points where the lace needed to be strengthened. Some bars did have one or two loops worked into them, and even second loops worked over the top of the first loop with two or three picots added, but, because the main motifs that formed the pattern were so heavily embossed with couronnes, the connecting bars were lost into the background.

Venetian Rose Point

This lace followed closely behind the Gros Point in the latter part of the sixteenth century. It was a luxury lace and the designs were the same in form as with the Gros Point but on a much smaller scale. The bars became part of the whole design and were three-way bars with small rings holding the three points together; every bar ring and picot had smaller picots decorating it.

Venetian Point de Neige

This followed at the end of the seventeenth century. The workmanship was beyond doubt at its peak at this stage, but the designs had become fussy. One feature of this lace was the layers of scallops minute versions of the edgings given in this book (*see p. 67*). All three edgings would be worked one on top of the other or overlapping either round the edge of rings or along the edge of couronnes. The bars used for the grounding had rings of scallops and picots at each intersection. The edgings of most Point de Neige were composed of miniature flowers, sometimes arranged in groups of three, or alternating one large flower with one small one. Each was bordered with two or three picots so small that today, after many washings, they can be mistaken for little knots in the thread, but under a magnifying glass it can be seen that they are bullion picots.

Spanish laces

These developed in the sixteenth and seventeenth centuries very much along the same lines as the Venetian Point, but were remarkable for the heavily ornamented bars, or *brides,* which formed part of the design. Very few variations on the stitches were used during this period. It was the use of couronnes and the raised edges, often with picots, that made this a 'crunchy', heavy lace. The cordonette was made to turn over at nearly every bend by using the method explained on p. 48.

Point d'Alençon and Point d'Argentan

Both Alençon and Argentan lace were worked in a very fine thread. Alençon had the outline of the design raised by close buttonhole stitch worked over a few threads, but there was not the carved look of the Italian laces. Bars were replaced by a mesh worked in rows from one motif to another. Argentan differed from Alençon in the way the mesh was worked. It had a hexagonal mesh, and each bar of the mesh was covered with a regular number of buttonhole stitches – usually ten to each side.

Point de France

A late seventeenth-century lace that did not have a raised outline to the motifs, but had a large number of couronnes added to emphasise the design, and all the scrolls were raised over a great many threads forming very solid areas in the lace.

Point de Gaze

Another extremely fine lace, made in Brussels at the end of the nineteenth century and into the early twentieth. It had spaced buttonhole stitch worked over the cordonnette. The main characteristic of this lace was the layered petals of the flowers and the number of different wheels worked into the centres of the flowers and also into the scrolls that form much of the design.

A Point de Venise cap owned by Pat Gibson

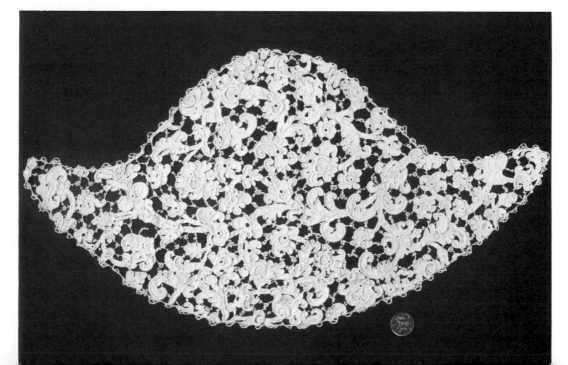

A blouse and collar, in the Point de Gaze style, designed and worked by Catherine Barley; the design is shown partially worked in *Creative Design in Needlepoint Lace*

This collar, worked by Ann Forbes-Cockell, is in the style of Point de Gaze, and is an interpretation of her original design shown in *Creative Design in Needlepoint Lace*

Burano Lace

This is the 'modern' Venetian lace, made from the mid-nineteenth century through to the first quarter of the twentieth. It is still made for the tourist trade. The fillings are numerous and wheels form quite a large part of the design. The outline of the design is raised.

FLAT LACES

Point Plat

This was worked in Venice from the late seventeenth century and was composed of rows of corded stitch worked in different directions, relieved with small areas worked in double Bruxelles stitch. Small holes were placed within the shape, formed by missing four or five stitches on one row then being worked back into the long loop in the return row. All bars were joined together at the intersections by small rings worked from one bar to another

One corner of a large tablecloth, size approximately 150 × 185 cm (60 × 84 in) showing cupids surrounded by scrolls. Owned by Catherine Barley, it is dated *c.* 1890 and is probably an example of Burano lace

all with picots worked into them. The edgings were the most intricate part of the lace, being worked in the same way as the edges of Rose Point and Point de Neige, little flowers sometimes in groups or alternating one small with a large one. Always remembering that 'large' in this case was extremely small.

Coralline Point

The story behind this lace tells of a girl whose sailor lover handed her a piece of coral before setting sail; in his absence she sat down and copied the coral with her needle. The edging of this lace was very like the first two patterns in this book (see pp.*48–49*), the difference being

15

Detail from centre of tablecoth

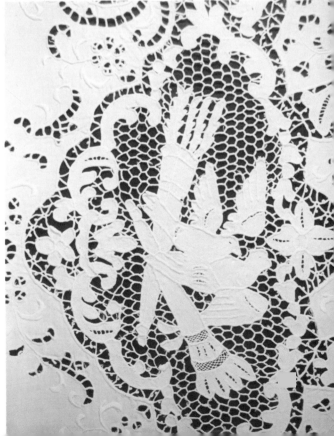

Another point of interest

An example of Youghal lace owned by Anne Aldrich; Youghal lace is the only true needlepoint lace of Ireland

that the size of the complete pattern on the Coralline Point was smaller than one loop of the patterns given here. There was no raised outline and the pattern meandered at will.

Point de Venise à Réseau

By the beginning of the eighteenth century, Venetian laces had been influenced by the lace of France and Flanders and gave birth to this particularly beautiful lace. It has very floral designs and a mesh, and its beauty comes from the diversity of the stitches. All the stitches given in this book could be found in one piece of this lace, plus many others, that are given in *Creative Design in Needlepoint Lace*. The

Part of a Youghal flounce from the collection belonging to Anne Aldrich

réseau was worked in straight lines from one motif across to another. Against the close texture of the stitches forming the pattern, the mesh was worked well spaced, forming a softer lace than the previous laces of Italy.

Youghal

This was the true Irish Needlepoint lace and was based on Point de Venise à Réseau. It

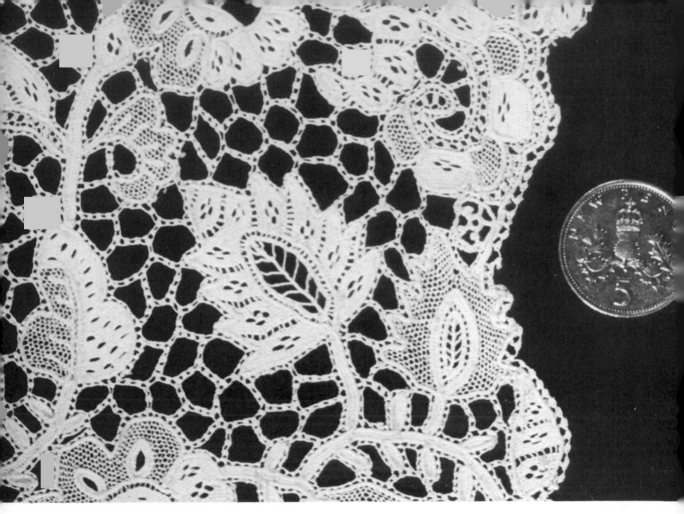

The flounce in close-up, showing the unusual bars

contained many of the stitches mentioned in the previous paragraph; the difference between the two laces was in the grounding: Youghal lace has a distinct ground of bars, each having the same number of picots worked into them. In both laces the outline is sometimes over-sewn, the stitches being neatly spaced.

TAPE LACES

Mixed lace first appeared in the seventeenth century and the Venetian Guipure was known as Mezzo Punto. Since then, they have been given many names, such as Royal Battenburg, Honiton Point, Duchess, Princes, Point de Bruges, Limoges and Ideal Honiton. Some of these are misleading, being associated with the names for bobbin laces. Tape lace had the same designs, fillings and raised work as Gros Point

but, instead of a cordonnet, there was a braid, made with bobbins, to a pattern traced out on parchment and worked on a pillow. The curves were made in the tape as it was worked.

There is still some doubt as to where this lace originated, but it is thought that it was probably in Naples and that it was introduced for the general public as an easier and cheaper form of the rich points produced by the aristocracy. Machine-made tapes were introduced at the beginning of the nineteenth century and were frowned upon by the traditional needle-point lacemakers. The designs became progressively more coarse, using thick thread and, by the mid-nineteenth century, printed glazed cloth patterns were sold that needed very little at all in the way of fillings. There was a different class of tape lace; Branscombe and Battenburg at the end of the nineteenth and beginning of the twentieth centuries were two forms that were beautifully executed and

intricate in design. But, in the July issue of *The Queen* 1899 there is the following passage:

> Overskirts to be worn this year are made in various patterns with braid lace and lace stitches. . . . The work is quite easy. It is correct to use a multiplicity of stitches of endless variety; but in lieu of these it is simply necessary to carry the thread from one point to another of the design and twist it, emphasising it here and there with wheels or with those raised circles made by twisting several strands of cotton round the point of scissors, buttonholing over them and then sewing them on where the pattern most requires them.

That, to my way of thinking, is a sepulchral monument to lace. I am sure that readers of this book can do much better than that, and it is

A tape lace collar with needlepoint fillings, worked by Mary Anderson

only time now before needlepoint lace is back in its rightful place.

ATTACHING LACE TO A GARMENT

The engrêlure

Needlepoint lace was always more expensive to produce than bobbin lace and so a narrow edge was worked using about 20 bobbins, making either a plain cloth band or what we now call cucumber stitch. This was attached to the top edge of the needlepoint lace and was always fixed with a running stitch so that it was easy to remove. It was this band that was sewn to the garment and was called the *engrêlure*. If this was damaged while transferring the lace from

A selection of tape lace motifs with various
needlepoint fillings, worked by Mary Anderson

20

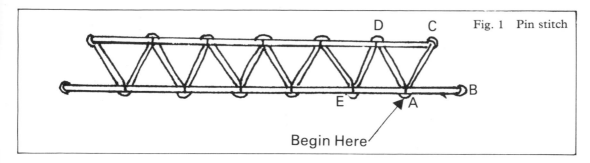

Fig. 1 Pin stitch

one garment to another it was easily replaced with another band of bobbin lace.

It is also possible to make a separate band to edge a collar, or similar, in needlepoint lace. Lay a cordonnet following the curve of the neckline that is being used. Work six rows of corded stitch. Then work one row where two stitches are worked into every other stitch; this will be the fold line. Then work a row making up the original number of stitches by putting a stitch into the loop between two stitches and two stitches into the loop made by the missed stitch. Follow with five more rows of corded stitch, working one stitch into each loop. Ladder stitch this band to the top of the finished collar.

Pin stitch

This is a neat and strong method of sewing on or inserting lace that is to be attached to material. The working proceeds from right to left, as a series of back stitches arranged as triangles. The movements are the same as faggot stitch or three-sided stitch, and an open effect is secured by using a large needle and fine thread.

To begin working, bring the needle out at A, put through at B and out at A. Repeat these movements once more. Put the needle in at A and out at D then in at A and out at E. Repeat all these former movements in this order successively.

The edges of the pieces to be joined are overlapped and the stitches are worked through two thicknesses. The fabric is cut away afterwards, close against the stitches. This stitch has the advantage of being independent of the warp or weft, so will work round a curve or along a straight edge just as effectively.

21

2.
Materials and Preparation

There are a number of things in favour of needlepoint lace, one of them being the ease of collecting together the necessary materials: sewing needles, the size depending on the thread being used, for the couching down of the outline of the design; ballpoint needles for working the lace stitches; background material to hold the work firm and to keep the tension right; a pattern, which needs to be covered with acetate film or the linen used in drawing offices; threads, of which there is such a variety that, for the practice runs on samplers, they will be found in most embroiderers' hideaways; thimbles are a must and a small pillow is a great help. Time is the only difficulty; that has always been hard to find, but this type of lace is soothing to do and a little like knitting in as much as there is always the urge to do one more row. There is no tying up of bobbins when the work is left and no fear of it being knocked over, with the risk of broken threads.

NEEDLES

A needle should always be slightly thicker than the thread being used, because it will make a hole in the material big enough for the thread to slip through easily. For the couching down of the design the following needles are suitable:

Betweens have a round eye and a No. 8 is about right when using machine sewing cotton;
Crewels have long eyes and a No. 10 is right for single strands of stranded sewing cotton or silks of a higher number than 100/3s;
Sharps No. 8 has a round eye; the needle is finer and longer than the No. 8 Betweens.

It is possible to purchase packets of mixed needles and, if a variety of threads is going to be used, then this is a good buy for beginners.

Ballpoint needles were first introduced to use with man-made stretch fabrics, but have proved their worth for working the needlelace stitches as they have blunt ends and small round eyes, whereas Tapestry needles have thick wide eyes that can spoil the lie of the close work.

THREADS

Threads for needlepoint lace can be as fine as you can find or thick and chunky, it really depends on the end product. For the samplers that follow, a Coton àBroder No. 30 was used for the outline (the cordonnet), while the lace stitches were worked in Coats Chain Mercer Cotton No. 40, which is sold in 20 g balls.

If the thread twists while working there are two things that can help. One is to take the needle down the thread to the stitches, then run the thread through the thumb and finger from the work up to the end of the thread. Secondly, make a point of using the thread as it runs off the spool, threading the needle before even cutting off the length. Another point: if the twist has formed a knot, place the tip of the needle into the loop and pull first one end and then the other away from the needle. This usually releases the knot, and a final sharp pull in both directions clears the thread.

THIMBLE

A thimble really is necessary, especially when couching, because of the layers of fabric that the needle has to go through; it is also useful when laying the top cordonnette because the needle has to find its way between closely packed stitches. It is quite painful once the needle has penetrated the top of the finger a number of times. If by chance blood is drawn

Needle lace worked by the author using some of her grandmother's 300 thread

The needlepoint pillow and stand is by Newnham Lace Equipment. The butterfly is being worked by the author and is from *Creative Design in Needlepoint Lace*

and gets on the work, roll a small ball of cotton wool or a small piece of bread, wet it with saliva and dab the stain; keep using a clean piece and fresh saliva and the stain will lift out.

PILLOWS

A pillow is necessary when using very fine threads, as it allows two hands to be free to manipulate the threads into position, but when using anything up to the equivalent of 80 crochet cotton it is not really needed, except to make you sit straight and to bring the work closer to your eyes. Pillows can be bought or can be made from a large round tin, such as those that contain babies' milk, dried potatoes or coffee. Fill the tin with dry sand, or something similar, to give added weight, replace the lid and wrap the tin in layers of wadding to allow for the insertion of pins. The diameter of

the pillow needs to be about 15 cm (6 in). Sew or tie the wadding in place, making sure it is tightly packed round the tin. Make a cover of dark coloured material allowing 2·5 cm (1 in) overlap each end. Run a line of tacking stitches round each end to draw up, and fasten off securely. Cut two circles of the material to fit top and bottom of the tin and turn under a small hem, then sew to each end.

THE PATTERN

The pattern or design can be taken from any diagram or photograph of old lace, but it can just as easily come from any other source, as will be seen in the chapter on design. The pattern is drawn on paper, which is then covered with acetate film or placed under draughtsman's linen. The acetate film is transparent with an adhesive backing which is covered with paper; the paper backing has to be peeled off before it is placed over and stuck to the design. Take care when applying the film as it will fly back with static electricity and will promptly stick itself to the wrong part of the design. Hold each end of the film with a finger and thumb and make a loop in the film, sticky side down. Lay this centre to the design and stick down from the centre to the outside edge, first to the right and then to the left. If the design has been drawn on tracing paper or tissue take care that the paper does not fly up to meet the acetate. Place the little fingers on the design and draw them out to the sides of the paper while laying the acetate down from the centre, as already explained. The reason for using the film is to stop the needle from piercing the paper on which the design is drawn; as it is smooth, the needle cannot pick up the hairs from the backing material. It has one drawback, and that is reflection when one is working under a light, and this is where the tracing linen has the advantage. The linen is more expensive but the same piece can be used more than once if working the same design but it has not the same reflective surface as the acetate. The linen does not have an adhesive backing; it is held in place by tacking threads round the outside of the design. Both products are available from drawing office suppliers and can be bought by the metre, or less in some places.

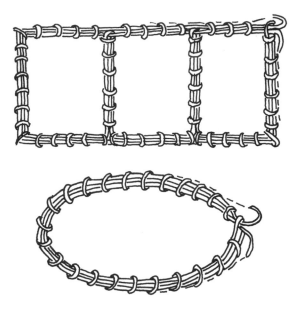

Fig. 2   Take a length of thread to be used as the cordonnet and fold in half. Thread a Sharps or Betweens needle with sewing cotton making a knot at one end. Bring the needle up through the backing material at the beginning of the design and through the loop of the thread being used for the cordonnet, and commence the couching

PREPARING THE BACKING MATERIAL

Originally a fine kid was used on which the design was traced. Then firms started producing patterns printed on glazed linen. These were issued by the thousands and can still be found in old collections and in antique shops. Now it is almost impossible to find even the glazed linen in the shops, except for some curtain linings, so calico has to replace it. Never use a wool-type backing, as the minute hairs get caught up in the working thread.

It is important to keep the colour of the material low key; the best colours are blue or green as they are restful to the eyes. Other plain colours can be used, but avoid patterned material.

The backing material is very important to the finished piece of lace. It has to be thick enough to give stability to the stitches as they are built up into the finished lace but, at the same time, pliable enough to handle. The backing needs to be three times the length of the design and just a little wider, plus turnings.

LAYING A CORDONNET

Before starting to lay the cordonnet, study the design to see how far the threads can be laid without having to cut off and rejoin. The cordonnet is always worked as a pair of threads laid side by side around the design, held in place with couching stitches.

To start, take twice the length of thread required, fold in half and the first couch stitch is taken through the loop of the fold. Both threads are then couched together as far as possible along the design. Use a needle with fine thread and make the stitches at regular intervals, keeping them about 3 mm ($\frac{1}{8}$ in) apart. Pull the stitches secure but not tight, otherwise the laid thread will have a wavy appearance. Keep the two threads parallel

25

while couching and do not allow them to pass over the top of each other. The threads must be held firm and taut while being couched down.

On reaching a point where there is a spur off the main run of the design, leave one thread behind. The other thread of the pair is taken along the spur, held at the end with a couching stitch and then folded back on itself and couched back beside its partner. The two threads continue side by side along the design until it is necessary to use just the one thread again.

At any point where the couched threads pass one of these spurs, on a return journey for instance, pass one or both threads through the little loop formed by the fold. In this way all parts of the design are locked together and there is no fear of the lace coming apart when taken off the backing material.

If using coloured threads for working the lace, use the same colour of sewing silk to couch with. Use fine-pointed needles for the couching and make sure the thread is taken through all layers of the backing material. The reason for this is that once the lace is finished, the couching stitches are cut between the layers of material, and the work just lifts off. The little cut ends of the couching can then be pulled out of the lace at the back. Some threads do get caught in the lace stitches and have to be cut close to the work. If the same colour has been used the little cut ends will not show.

If a new thread has to be joined in, leave the short thread out and lay a new thread in its place beside the other original thread. Make four or five couching stitches, then pull the new thread gently through until the end is just secured under the stitches; continue to lay the original one of the pair with the thread. Never let both threads run out close together, always allow at least 5 cm (2 in) of new thread to run alongside an existing thread.

When reaching the end of the design, take one thread through the loop made in the fold of the thread at the start, fold it over on itself and whip it back to the two laid threads for about 2·5 cm (1 in). Take the couching thread through the backing, make it secure and cut off. The other thread of the pair is continued over the pair at the start of the design, whipped as before and the couching thread is taken through the backing and finished off. The two ends of the laid thread are now cut off as close as possible.

The prepared material with the design is now laid on the pillow and held in place by pinning all four corners. The material must hold secure while the work is in progress so pin along both sides if necessary.

3.
The Stitches

There is only one stitch employed in needle-point lace – the looped buttonhole stitch – but the variety of ways in which it is used is almost endless, and even the recognised way of working any particular stitch can look completely different when worked by different people. Maybe there is one twist too many, or it is twisted in the opposite direction. Sometimes the tension is wrong for the stitch in question but, because the whole sampler has been worked in this way, the student has her own version of a sixteenth-century stitch that looks perfectly right. When this happens, keep that version and go back later to try the original.

The most simple stitches are given in this book, but they are the most important stitches to start with. They are, in the main, reproductions of genuine, old, hand-made needlepoint lace. Some of the old laces were unpicked stitch by stitch to find out how they were originally constructed. The stitches are given in order of simplicity of working and the first stitches are well within the limits of anyone who can thread a needle; the working instructions are precise and, for those who prefer to work from drawings, these are shown on a scale large enough to follow easily without the need of the written instructions.

The stitches in needlepoint lace are used in three different ways: for the fillings, for the grounds and for the couronnes. The main parts of the design are always worked in close stitches. These are the stitches that are whipped or corded and placed close together. The fillings between the design can be composite stitches that give an open-work effect. The fillings are endless and only the more common ones will be given here. This does not mean that the finished article need be any the less beautiful; the Venetian laces, when they were at their best in the sixteenth century, used quite simple stitches: corded stitch, Gros Point diamonds, veins and the Venetian stitches in single, double and treble formation.

There are a number of grounds: sometimes the lace motifs are held together with woven bars (or *brides*), or the bars can be twisted; sometimes the bars are buttonholed for their entire length (*brides claires*) or decorated with picots, loops and purls (*brides ornées*); sometimes, when the lace has smaller motifs and needs more background to hold it together, a mesh is worked of spaced buttonhole stitches.

This chapter covers the stitches, bars and meshes used for the fillings and ground; there will be a separate chapter on the workings of the couronnes because these too have many variations. They make a finished piece of lace into something special, but they are not vital, and many laces are worked without any raised work being added.

WORKING SAMPLES

Before beginning a lace pattern, always work a sample piece first, to practise the different stitches and to check the tension. For working the samplers it is convenient to have the finished piece of material in the region of 15 × 10 cm (6 × 4 in). This gives enough room for three different stitches, each in a block 5 × 7·5 cm (2 × 3 in) which is the area needed to get the right tension and rhythm for most stitches.

There are two ways in which a sampler can be prepared: either a cordonnet can be laid (*see p. 27*) in the form of three rectangles, or very narrow tape can be used sewn down each long side, with two short pieces dividing the length into three spaces. Prepare at least three pieces

A set of church vestments worked by Mary Anderson worked in 80 crochet cotton. Here the altar frontal ...

in either of these ways ready to practise the most frequently used stitches before starting on a design.

The first sampler will have the Bruxelles stitch worked as a close mesh (*see p. 31*), then the same stitch will be whipped and corded (*see p. 34*). These are the stitches used for filling in the solid areas of a pattern.

The second sampler will show the spaced, double and treble Bruxelles stitches (*see p. 34*), while the third will be three variations on the pea stitch (*see p. 37*). Any visit to Bruges will show lace displayed in most shop windows made entirely from these stitches so, having mastered them, one can expect to be able to work a piece of lace.

Working samplers with straight edges will not be of much use when confronted with a design that has scrolls and curves, with shapes trailing away to very narrow bands or exploding into large circles. So, a sampler of ovoid shapes should be worked to show how to

gain or lose stitches. If too many stitches are added, the lace will not lie flat but will become fluted, or the stitches will become so packed that the large shape of the stitch will be lost. The opposite will happen if too few stitches are made to the row; the lace will be weak, with the stitch pattern being stretched beyond recognition. Remember, a stitch is as wide as it is high and a space is the width of a stitch.

INCREASING AND DECREASING

To increase or decrease, new stitches are worked into the cordonnet at the end of the rows. If working a stitch pattern, then, depending on the number of stitches needed for the increase, the pattern has to be kept correct on these added stitches. Count back to the start of the last pattern block and work the new pattern into the freshly laid foundation stitches. This is easy when continuing along a line, but when the new foundation stitches are at the beginning of a row it is sometimes easier to work out a graph with pencil and paper. When working any of the whipped or corded stitches, the increases are worked on the end of the stitch line one way, and the next row is a corded one.

... the veil ...

... and the burse; the same design as the veil, but fronted on to gold kid

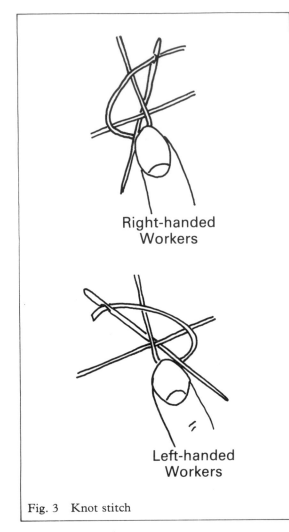

Right-handed Workers

Left-handed Workers

Fig. 3   Knot stitch

At the other side of the work, if extra stitches are required, make a knot stitch (*see p. 30*) on the cordonnet, add the extra stitches as required into the cordonnet, and twist under and over the cordonnet on this side before returning on the next row. On the next row, work into the new stitches just formed and, on reaching the knot stitch, start working over the loops of the previous row and the thread of the cording or whipped stitch in the usual way.

To make a knot stitch, lay the working thread under the thumb and make a buttonhole stitch, taking the needle under the couched thread and over the new working thread (*fig. 3*).

FILLINGS AND GROUNDS

Basic buttonhole (single Bruxelles) stitch

Once the foundation thread, the cordonnet, is laid, all stitches are worked independently of the backing material and at no point should the working thread be taken through it. The working thread starts on the side of the sampler where the work is to commence by being taken through four of the stitches holding the cordonnet. A knot stitch will hold the thread in position.

Work the first row of stitches, each one lying comfortably beside its neighbour not actually touching, but neither must there be enough room for a stitch to lie between them. Hold the thread down with the left thumb (right thumb, if you are left-handed), put the needle under the cordonnet, and pull the needle through. The length of thread is then wrapped round the little finger of the right hand (left hand, if you are left-handed), while the thumb and first finger hold the thread close to the work and the stitch is carefully pulled into place. By pulling to the right or to the left, the stitch will fall close to, or spaced from, the previous stitch. (Worked side by side it forms the toilé which is the pattern of the lace, as distinct from the grounds. To work the ground, or *réseau*, the stitch is spaced evenly, connecting one part of the pattern to another and forming a mesh.) It is not easy to keep the tension correct, but with practice it will become automatic, and if this way of working is used from the start, speed will be the bonus that follows. As the working thread gets shorter, the need to wrap it round the little finger diminishes and a very short thread can be pulled through and placed in position in one movement. The first row is worked over the cordonnet, along the top of the space being filled. On reaching the end of the row, whip the thread round the cordonnet at the side of the panel or design then work a stitch into the the loops formed between two stitches and continue working the second row into the loops formed by the first row.

Apart from when increasing or decreasing keep the number of stitches the same on each row. It takes two stitches to make a loop, so, if the first row is made up of ten stitches, there

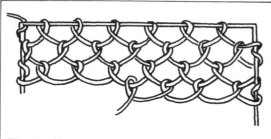

Fig. 4   Single Bruxelles stitch

Usually, if the thread is one and three-quarter times the length of the row to be worked, it is safe to start working across the line; if the thread is less, it is not worth taking a chance, so start with a new thread. It sometimes seems a waste of thread, but it will save the time it would take to unpick the row; it will also save a lot of frustration. The new thread is joined in by running through the four couching stitches, in the same way as if just starting, and will be held in place by a knot stitch. The end of the old thread should be taken through four couched stitches in the opposite direction to the new thread and cut off. Do not discard cut-off ends of thread; they can be used for padding out the thick parts of the cordonnette.

will be nine loops between stitches, but there will be the two loops at each end of the row made between the cordonnet and the first and last stitches. To keep the ten stitches in each row, miss the first loop made between the cordonnet and the first stitch, but work into ten loops, which takes in the last loop between stitch and cordonnet. If this is done on each row the ten stitches will remain constant.

This same Bruxelles stitch can be used in pairs or trebles, and in all these formations can be whipped or corded. It is also the basis of the pea stitch and all its variations, so it is the most versatile stitch to start with. Its beauty depends completely on the evenness and regularity of the working.

Work backward and forward over the area being filled, always keeping the stitches the correct height, the correct spacing and the correct tension.

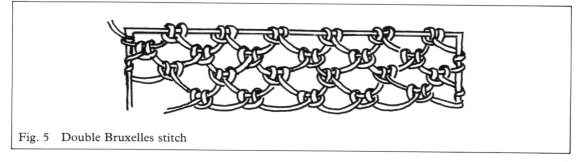

Fig. 5   Double Bruxelles stitch

Double Bruxelles stitch

Row 1 Work two stitches close together over the cordonnet, then miss a space equal to the width of the two stitches and make the next pair of stitches. Continue across the row until reaching the cordonnet at the side of the design. Take the thread under and over the cordonnet twice.

Row 2 Place two stitches into each loop between the pairs of the previous row. To keep the numbers constant in each row miss the first loop between the last stitch and the cordonnet.

INCREASING AND DECREASING

Increases should be made at the end of a row by working the number of extra stitches needed to fill the space. Then, on working back along the next row, work the pairs of stitches to keep the pattern correct. On an increase row, two stitches should be worked into the loop between the last stitch and the cordonnet of the previous row, otherwise a gap will appear in the pattern. Decrease where necessary by working along the row until there is no room to place another pair of stitches, make a knot stitch into the cordonnet and return along the next row.

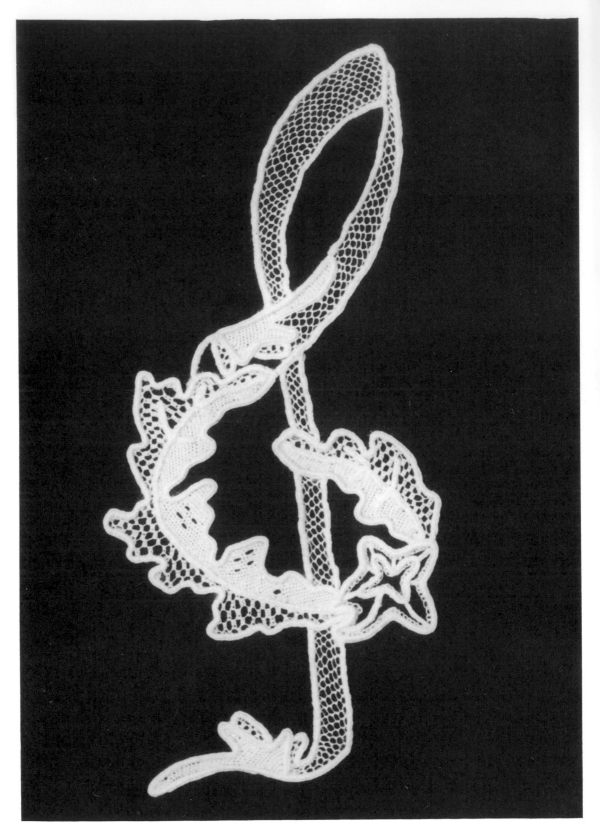

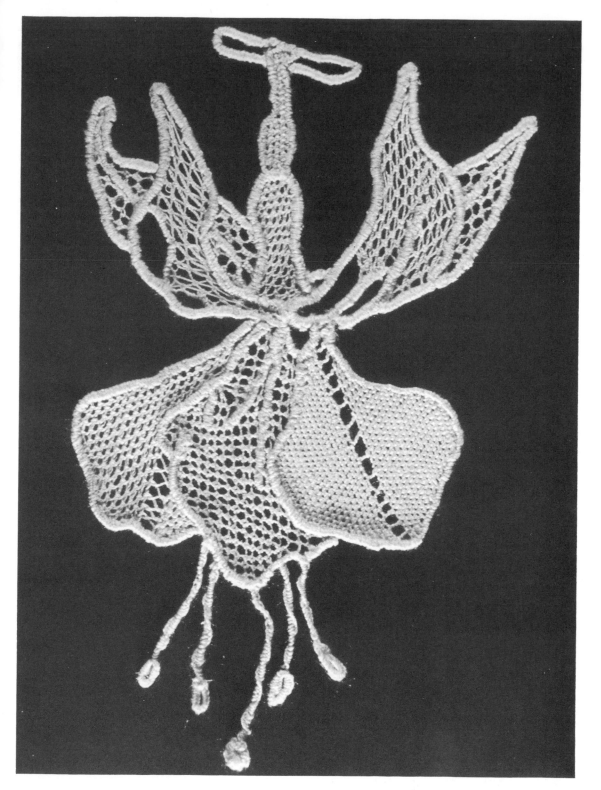

Treble clef, designed and worked by Mary-Ellen Tunnell using 150 Unity cotton

A fuschia, designed and worked by Vera Nichols; her first piece of needlepoint lace

Treble Bruxelles stitch

The same rules apply to this stitch; it must be worked at the right tension, each stitch the same size as its neighbour, and the spaces between the stitches must remain a constant length. The space should be equal to the width taken by the three stitches.

Start along the top cordonnet, working a row of groups of three stitches with the corresponding space of the three stitches between the groups. Take the thread under and over the cordonnet at the side of the design twice. Make the first group of three stitches in the loop between the last groups of the first row.

Because this filling covers quite an area along each row, work even and odd numbers of blocks alternately. The illustration shows four groups on the first row, three groups on the second row, then back to four groups on the third row. In this way the edges remain straight.

INCREASING
To increase, add an extra one, two or three stitches as needed to fill the space, and then work back along the next row incorporating the new stitches into the pattern.

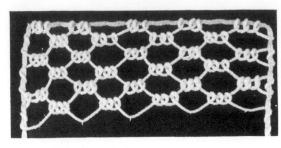

Treble Bruxelles stitch

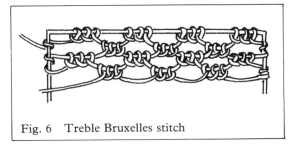

Fig. 6   Treble Bruxelles stitch

Corded stitch

Row 1   Work the row of buttonhole stitches along the top of the space. Take the working thread under and over the cordonnet at the side and take it across to the beginning of the row. The laid thread should be lying along the bottom of the loops of the first row. Take the thread under and over the cordonnet *twice*.

Row 2   Work the first stitch of the second row over the loop between the first two stitches of the first row and the laid thread. Continue across the row. Miss the loop between the last stitch and the cordonnet of the first row. Take the thread under and over the cordonnet *once* and lay it back along the base of the stitches just worked. The thread is now taken under and over the cordonnet *twice*.

Row 3   Make the first stitch of the third row into the loop formed between the cordonnet and the first stitch of the previous row; the last stitch of the row is worked into the loop

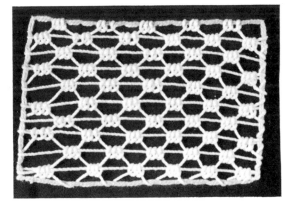

Corded treble Bruxelles stitch

between the last stitch of the previous row and the cordonnet. Take the thread under and over the cordonnet *once*.

Row 4 Work the second row again.

Keep to the sequence of these four rows to keep the edges straight. When working with the right hand, start the stitches at the right hand top corner and cord back from left to right. If working with the left, hand, start the stitches at the left hand corner and cord back from right to left.

INCREASING

If increasing, work the extra stitches on a buttonhole row either at the beginning or the end of the row.

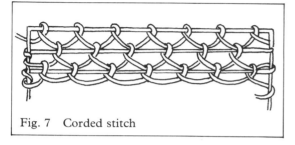

Fig. 7   Corded stitch

Whipped treble Bruxelles stitch

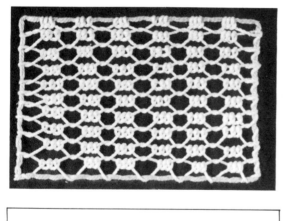

Whipped stitch

Row 1 Work a row of stitches along the top of the space, take the thread under and over the cordonnet at the side *once*. Take the needle under and over the loop between the stitches of the first row back to the starting point. Go over and under the cordonnet *once*, but down to the depth of the second row.

Row 2 Miss the loop of the cordonnet and the first stitch and make the stitches of the second row into the loops only of the previous row; go under and over the cordonnet *once* and whip back as before.

Row 3 The first stitch of the third row is worked into the loop between the cordonnet and the first stitch of the previous row.

As the stitches are again being worked in one direction only, the same rule applies for left and right handers as the previous stitch.

INCREASING AND DECREASING

Increase and decrease on the buttonhole row, either at the beginning or the end of the row, and whip back over all the stitches.

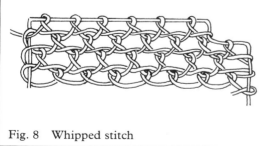

Fig. 8   Whipped stitch

Whipped stitch variations

The buttonhole stitches of the second and following rows can be worked over both the whipped thread and the loops between stitches, which will give a tighter effect. Alternatively, the buttonhole stitches can be worked into the whipped thread only. This gives a much more open filling. This second version is not recommended for large areas.

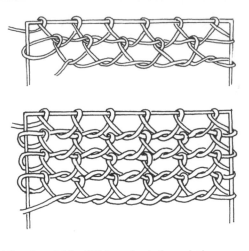

Figs 9 and 10   Whipped stitch variation

Pea stitch

For the following composite stitch patterns take the thread under and over the cordonnet at the beginning and end of each row.

Row 1   Work a row of buttonhole stitches in pairs with a spacing of two buttonhole stitches between each pair.

Row 2   Work one stitch into each long loop between each pair of stitches of the first row.

Row 3   Work two stitches into each long loop.

Pea stitch variation 1

Row 1   Work a row of pairs of stitches with a space of four stitches between each pair.

Row 2   Work four stitches into each long loop.

These alternate rows form the pattern. Keep the number of stitches in each individual row the same if the sides are to be kept straight.

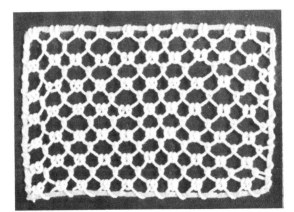

Pea stitch

INCREASING AND DECREASING

All increasings and decreasings should be taken into the pattern in the following way. If on reaching the end of the row the space is too small to include all four stitches on the alternate rows, just add two or three stitches to fit comfortably into the extra space. Take the thread under and over the cordonnet twice. Then form a short loop to lay under the extra stitches. On the return row the two stitches of the even rows will fit into the shortened end loop. If other stitches are still called for to enlarge the curve even further, again add the extra stitches. Then work in these stitches to keep the continuity of the pattern. The same thing applies if adding stitches at the beginning of a row.

Decrease as many stitches as necessary either end of the row, forming a smaller loop before or after working round the cordonnet. Then add into this first or last loop only as many stitches as will fit the loop at the right tension. Again, keep the pattern correct over the main part of the filling.

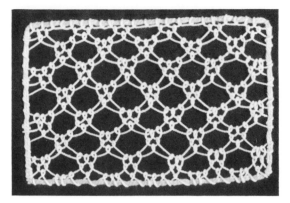

Pea stitch, second variation

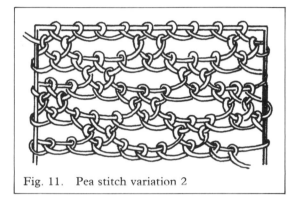

Fig. 11.   Pea stitch variation 2

Pea stitch variation 2

This is the prettiest pea stitch variation.

Row 1   Work a row of buttonhole stitches across the top of the cordonnet, equally spaced.

Row 2   Work a stitch into the first two loops of the top row, miss two loops and place a stitch into the next two loops. Continue in this way across the space. Take the thread under and over the cordonnet at the side of the work.

Row 3   Place one stitch on the loop between the pairs of stitches of row 2 and work three stitches into each long loop.

Row 4   Make a long loop under the one stitch between the pairs of row 2, then work one stitch into each of the two loops formed by the group of three stitches of row 3.

Repeat row 3, working three stitches into each long loop and one stitch on the loop between the pairs of stitches. The pattern is formed by repeating rows 3 and 4.

Pea variation 3

This filling is only more complicated in that there are extra rows to form the pattern which includes a corded thread and a new stitch. Take it slowly; don't stop in the middle of the practice run and you will find it to be quite straightforward.

Row 1   Work a row of pairs of stitches with a space of four stitches between each pair.

Row 2   Work two stitches into each long loop. At the end of the row take the thread under and over the cordonnet and cord back, laying the thread directly under the loops of the previous row, now under and over the cordonnet on the opposite side.

Row 3   Work over the loops of the previous row and the corded thread as follows: work two stitches into the long loop, one stitch between the pair of stitches on row 2 and then two

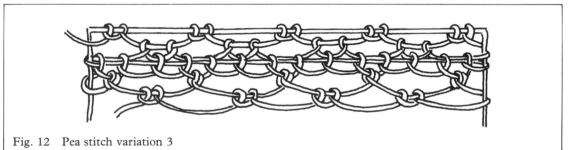

Fig. 12   Pea stitch variation 3

stitches into the next long loop. Continue in this way across the row.

Row 4 This brings in another stitch not yet worked; it is called *point de Sorrento* and instructions and diagram are below.

The Sorrento stitch is worked on the loop between the pairs of stitches of the previous row. Make a long loop under the single stitch of the previous row. Then work another Sorrento stitch on the loop between the next pair of stitches as before.

Row 5 Work two stitches over each long loop of row 4, and cord back.

Repeat from row 2.

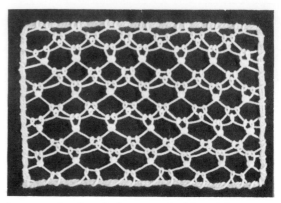

An example of a stitch pattern looking right even though it does not follow the pattern; the corded row has been omitted

Point de Sorrento

There is a legend to this stitch. A small child on the Isle of Capri was in trouble at school because she could not keep the tension of her buttonhole stitch correct. As the other children ran off home the poor little one had to stay behind. It was getting dark and she was becoming very hungry, so she decided to knot each stitch to make it stay in place, praying Signora would not notice. Needless to say, Signora did, but was so impressed with the stitch, that it was taken back to Sorrento and placed into the curriculum of her lace school. It became a traditional Italian lace stitch in the eighteenth century, and can be found in the lace made at Burano up until the turn of this century.

Row 1 Work a buttonhole stitch over the cordonnet, then take the thread back over the buttonhole stitch and bring the needle through the loop of the stitch.

Row 2 to end Work this stitch over the loop of the previous row.

When used as a filling this stitch can be corded or whipped. It must not be pulled tight when working or it will form a knot and the beauty of the stitch is lost.

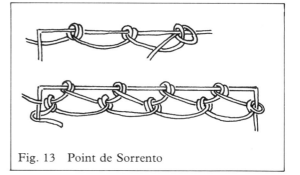

Fig. 13   Point de Sorrento

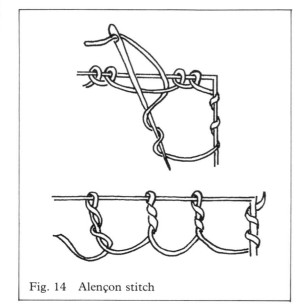

Fig. 14   Alençon stitch

Church lace stitch

The introduction of crochet lace as an industry dates back to the beginning of the nineteenth century. A Mademoiselle Riego de la Blanchardière discovered that a particular type of Spanish lace could be copied effectively with a crochet hook. The needlepoint lace stitches that inspired the double and treble stitches of *filet* or *lacis* crochet worked for the Church was this next stitch pattern.

Rows 1–3   Work three rows of close buttonhole stitches, working into every loop. Check that the number of stitches remains the same on each row.

Row 4   This is worked in Alençon stitch. To work this stitch, take the needle under and over the loops between two stitches, then form a twist on the working thread by taking the needle twice under and over the loop just made. Miss four stitches (three loops) of the previous row, then work another Alençon stitch. Continue across the row. Take the thread under and over the cordonnet at the side of the space.

Row 5   Work four close buttonhole stitches into each long loop between the Alençon stitches.

Rows 6 and 7   Work one stitch into each loop of the previous row.

The following instructions are all very simple and are the fillings used extensively in Tape Laces of all kinds. The stitch used is still the Point de Bruxelles, but the precise groupings give quite different effects.

Point d'Anvers

This filling was often used in Limoges lace, which was a form of tape lace that had no openwork edge; the worker had to work buttonhole stitch all round the inside edge of the tape before she could start the fillings.

Row 1   Over the top cordonnet make one stitch, leave a space of three stitches and make three stitches. Continue to leave a space and work three until reaching the end of the row; work two stitches and take the thread round the side cordonnet twice.

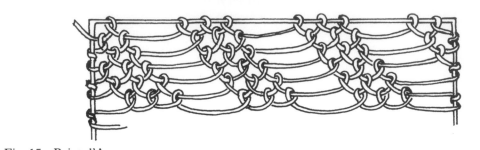

Fig. 15   Point d'Anvers

Row 2   Start by making one stitch between the stitches of the last pair of row 1. Leave a space of three stitches then make the first stitch of the block of three into the long loop, then one stitch into the next two loops of the three stitches of row 1. Continue across the space to the first stitch of row 1 and make one stitch each side of it. Take the thread round the cordonnet twice.

The blocks of stitches progress one stitch to the right on each row, adding the extra stitches at the start of a row on the left-hand side and leaving the stitches out at the end of a row on the right.

Spider Web filling

Work a small sampler first; the depth of the loop must remain constant and, when tracing off the pattern, it is best to mark the pin positions before starting the work. For the best effect, the two sides of the long loop should equal the length taken up by the group of five buttonhole stitches. Leave the pins in the work while working the sampler until the next row is worked each time. When reaching the end of each row, anchor into the cordonnet at the right depth to keep the pattern constant; this will be in line with the row of pins.

Row 1   Start at the top left-hand side of the top cordonnet by knotting in the working thread. Make a loop by placing the pin in position, taking the thread under the pin head and up to the top cordonnet, and work five close buttonhole stitches over the cordonnet. Make the next loop around the pin in the same way and work the next group of five close buttonhole stitches; continue across the space.

Row 2   Take the working thread down the cordonnet on the right-hand side to the depth

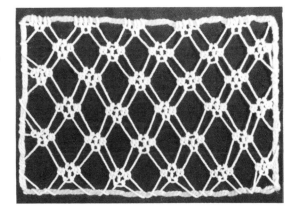

Spider Web filling

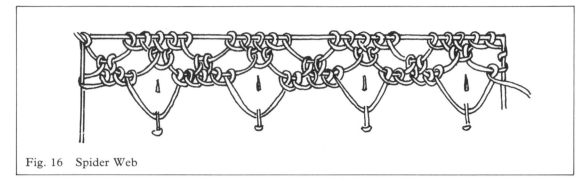

Fig. 16 Spider Web

of the line of pins. Take the needle up and make two stitches into the centre loops of the group of five stitches, i.e. one each side of the centre stitch of the group. Make one stitch each side of the pin holding the long loop, then make two stitches into the centre loops of the next block of five stitches, and so on across the row.

Row 3 Make two stitches to the left of the pair held by the pin, remove the pin and place one stitch between the pair, then make two stitches to the right of the pair. This is equivalent to the group of five stitches on the first row. Take the thread down and round the pin placed as in row 1, and make the next block of five stitches – two into the loop to the left of the pair, one between the pair held by the pin, and two to the right of the pair on the loop. Continue across the row in this way.

On reaching the side cordonnet, take the working thread down the cordonnet to the depth of the pins and repeat row 2.

Variation on Flemish lace stitch

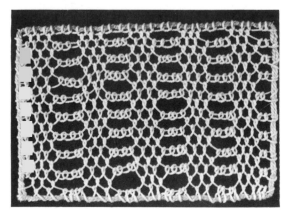

Flemish lace sitch

Row 1 Over the top cordonnet work two stitches, leave a space of two, then work another two stitches. Leave the space of six, work another pair, leave the space of two and work another pair, then leave the space of six. Continue in this way across the area being filled; try to end with two pairs of stitches if possible.

Row 2 Place two stitches on the loops between the pairs of the previous row and work six stitches over the long loops.

These two rows form the pattern.

Point Brabançon

This is very close to the Flemish stitch.

Row 1 Leave a loop equivalent to three stitches, make a stitch over the top cordonnet, leave a space of one stitch then make another stitch. Continue across the area with the space of three then the two spaced stitches.

Row 2 Work three stitches on the long loop and one stitch between the pairs on the first row.

These two rows form the pattern.

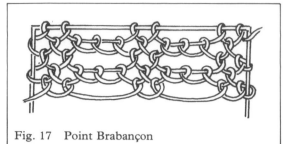

Fig. 17   Point Brabançon

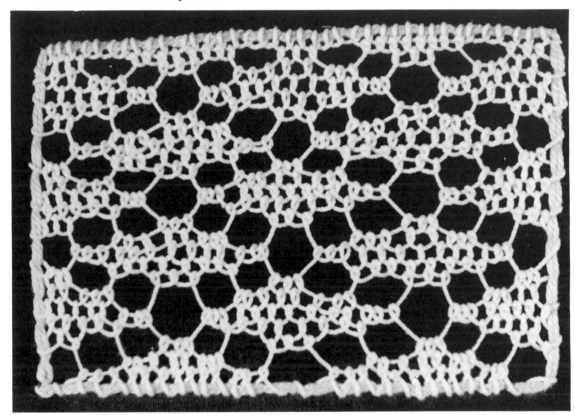

Gros Point Diamonds Gaze Quadrillée (see *Creative Design in Needlepoint Lace*, p. 92). Some students find this stitch easier to follow from the photograph than from written instructions

BARS

Bars, or *brides,* are the connecting threads thrown across a space to strengthen any weak points in the lace. Sometimes the bars are part of the design and are drawn into the pattern; often they are added at the discretion of the worker. The bars are worked before the final cordonnette is laid in any raised work (*see p. 44*). Lace without the raised work would be held together with a background mesh; the design would not be heavy enough to hold together with just the bars. Some of the

42

modern lace made in Burano has a firm mesh at the neckline of a collar, for instance, then trails off into a background of bars around the outer edge. Most lace can be identified by its grounding because each area had its own individual method of construction. Bars were time-consuming and, therefore, costly to produce, and gradually gave way to meshes, but all the earliest lace was connected by bars, and there were many ways in which they were worked.

To form a bar

Throw a thread from A on the left to B on the right, then back to A and to B again. Buttonhole stitch together the laid threads, with or without the picots shown in the following pages.

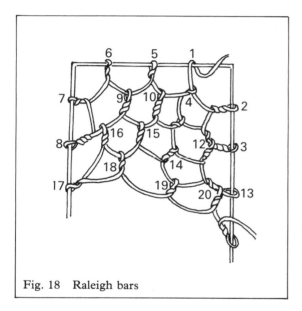

Fig. 18   Raleigh bars

Raleigh (branching) bars

When a large expanse of background is needed it is necessary to lay a foundation to work over. The bars are then called Raleigh or branching bars and are worked across the top right-hand corner; the foundation threads work from top to side in the form of a triangle. It is important to twist the threads once, twice or even three times in places to allow the foundation to lie flat once the buttonhole stitches are worked. By following the diagram from 1 to 17 the rest of the work should follow easily.

Buttonhole the thread in the same order, starting at 1 down to the twist at 2. Take the working thread over to 2 and buttonhole back to the end of the twist, pick up the loop of the last stitch from the group of stitches worked down from 1. Take the needle through from underneath the stitch as this keeps the stitches flat.

Work the buttonhole stitches down to the start of the twist before reaching 3. Twist the working thread round the foundation thread to 3 then buttonhole back to the start of the twist at 4.

Take the working thread across and pick up a loop of a stitch on the first bar made and work back to the start of the twist at 5.

Take the thread up and over the cordonnet then buttonhole to the start of the twist at 6.

Take the thread up to the cordonnet as at 5 and buttonhole down to the start of the twist at 7.

Continue in this way, remembering to pick up the loop of the stitch on each of the previous bars on passing, always under, up and through the loop to keep the bar lying flat. Picots can be worked at regular intervals along the bars.

Alençon bars

The bars are worked using two opposite rows of buttonhole stitches. Take the working thread over and down through the top loop, then take the needle through the bottom loop from behind; now make three more loops in the same way into the same space.

Keep the threads flat, do not allow them to lie one on top of the other. Bring the thread over and under the top loop and twist four or five times round the bar just made to the base. Take the thread under and over the bottom loop and whip along the bottom edge to the position of the next bar and repeat.

Alençon beads

Alençon beads are composed of the three loops made between top and bottom edges of the lace in the same way, but are left untwisted. When the rows of beads have been worked, run the back of the thumb nail down each block to make them lie flat.

PICOTS

When used as long straight points to enrich the raised cordonnette, they were called Spines, Thorns or *Fleurs Volantes*. Some laces, especially those made in the Alençon area of France, were edged with loop picots. They were so small and worked so close together that they looked like a ragged edge. But on close inspection one can only wonder at the effect they must have had on the eyesight of the workers. However, that was lace of the late seventeenth century; now in the twentieth century the fine thread is no longer available to us. The picots can be worked along the edge of the cordonnette (*see p. 45*), inside and outside edges of rings, or either at intervals or closely spaced either side of bars.

To work a picot

Work from right to left along to the position of the first picot, place a pin under the foundation threads of the bar and into the base material; if working on a pillow, stick the pin into the pillow itself. Pass the working thread from right to left under the pin then, still working to the left, over the top of and down behind the bar. Throw the working thread over the point

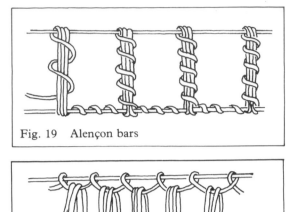

Fig. 19   Alençon bars

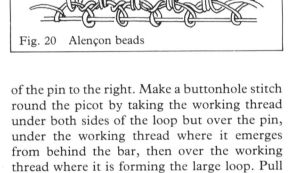

Fig. 20   Alençon beads

of the pin to the right. Make a buttonhole stitch round the picot by taking the working thread under both sides of the loop but over the pin, under the working thread where it emerges from behind the bar, then over the working thread where it is forming the large loop. Pull tight to form the picot.

Always work a buttonhole stitch after a picot to hold it in position. The spacing of the picots will depend on the number of button-hole stitches worked between each picot. The length of each can be varied by the placing of the pin to form a scalloped edge.

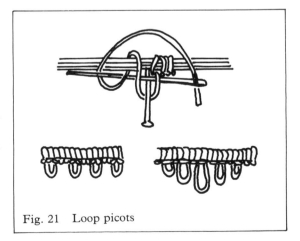

Fig. 21   Loop picots

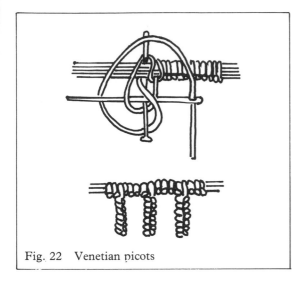

Fig. 22   Venetian picots

Venetian picots

These picots look best if all are worked the same length, so count the number of buttonhole stitches placed up to the loop of the first picot and repeat this number each time.

Work the buttonhole stitches from right to left along the bar to the position of the first picot. Place the pin under the foundation threads into the base material or into the pillow, as for the previous picot, to the length required. Take the working thread round the pin, make a buttonhole stitch over the bar, taking the thread down and under the pin for the second time from right to left. Throw the thread in a loop over the top of the bar and to the right-hand side of the picot. Now take the needle over the right-hand side of the first loop, under the working thread, over the pin, under the left-hand side of the loop and over the working thread. Pull the thread tight at the pin head forming the end of the picot, then buttonhole up the rest of the loop to the bar.

Continue to buttonhole along the bar threads to the position of the next picot. The number of stitches between and also the number of stitches that form the picot length must remain constant or the edge will look untidy.

Purls

These picots can be worked directly into the edge loop of the cordonnette stitches, spaced evenly into every other one or two loops.

To work the purls, make a buttonhole stitch leaving a loop the length of the purl, throw the working thread to the right then down and round to the left. Place the needle behind the buttonhole stitch and through the loop formed by the working thread. Place the thumb nail on the end of the loop of the purl and pull tight to form a knot. Keep all purls the same length and work at least one buttonhole stitch between each purl.

VEINS

The Venetian laces are composed of very few different stitches, the leaves nearly always being worked in corded or close Bruxelles stitch. Through the centre of the leaves a row of small holes are placed to represent the veins.

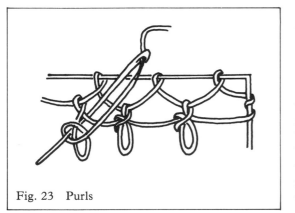

Fig. 23   Purls

Working a leaf from top to bottom

Work across the leaf to the centre, making a stitch into each loop of the previous row. Miss the centre stitch then work to the other side of the leaf working into every loop as before. If using corded stitch take the thread back and on the next stitch row, work to the centre make two stitches into the long loop and continue to the other side. If working the Bruxelles stitch the two stitches would be placed on the long loop on the return row. With either stitch, work two or three rows and then make another hole directly under the first in the same way. Continue down the leaf to the base making a hole at the centre on every second or third row.

Working a leaf from side to side

Work through to the centre of the leaf and make a row of holes in the following manner. Work into two loops and miss one loop along the length of the leaf, cord back if using corded stitch. Then on the following row work one stitch into each short loop and two stitches into each long loop. Do this on the return row if working the Bruxelles stitch.

Working a diagonal row of holes (starting from left or right)

Work into the first two loops and then miss a loop, then work into each loop across the row. On the next stitch row make two stitches into each long loop and one stitch into each short loop. Work two rows. On the next row work into four loops, miss one, then work across to the end of the row. On the next stitch row make two stitches into the long loop. Continue to work down the leaf moving two stitches across the line to make the hole.

Working a diagonal row of holes (starting from right to left)

To make the hole move in the opposite direction, work across the row to the last three stitches, miss a loop, then work into the last two loops. On the next stitch row work two stitches into the long loop. Work two rows. Make the next hole by working across the row to the last five loops, miss a loop, and work into the last four loops. Continue moving the hole towards the centre by missing a loop, two loops in, on each equivalent row.

Working a series of diagonal lines

A series of diagonal lines, one under the other can be worked down a leaf by repeating the above instructions on the sixth row down from the first two holes worked in the leaf. It will mean that at some time during the working of the leaf there might be four holes being worked on one line; it will depend on the number of stitches being used to fill the leaf.

It is quite possible that the leaves would only be long enough to place one set of holes, especially with the shaping of the leaf, as there would not be enough stitches to give the space for more. A small leaf would look better with a central vein running from top to bottom.

Antique lace very enlarged to show the buttonhole bars with picots. The Spanish Columns in the centre of the motif are explained in *The Technique of Needlepoint Lace* (p. 79) and the petals are made very simply using the Four Hole Diamond explained on p. 69 of *Creative Design in Needlepoint Lace*

4.
Raised Work

The texture of the lace can vary from extreme delicacy when worked in fine threads to an opulent profusion of raised work and couronnes.In fact it can look as if it has been carved, and at one point in its history was referred to as *Scolipto in Relievo*. The following words are translated from *Elegia Sopra un Collaretto* by Agnolo Firanzuola (*c.* 1520):

> The collar was sculptured by my lady
> In bas reliefs such as arachne
> And she who conquered her could ne'er excel,
> Look at that lovely foliage, like an acanthus.

It is the cordonnette, together with the couronnes, which gives the lace the appearance of carved work.

WORKING THE CORDONNETTE

The cordonnette follows the same route as the cordonnet but is worked after all the lace stitches are finished and before the lace is removed from the backing material. Generally a cordonnette is used in conjunction with bars or *brides* and strengthens the edges of all motifs. It helps keep the lace in its original shape. Once washed and pressed the use of an afficot (an instrument used for polishing the raised parts of the lace) will lift all the edges and remove any 'kinks' that appear round the outside edge of the buttonhole stitch.

Two or four strands of the same thread as used for the stitches will be sufficient for the laid thread of any lace that is to be used for underwear or babies clothes. Collars, cuffs, bags, or any household goods can be raised to the extent of looking as if they had been sculptured. The photograph of the design worked by

Catherine Barley gives an idea of the number of threads needed to get a really good padding.

Try a sample piece first to get the sweep of the wide curved areas that are then reduced to a whisper. When the lace was first produced in this way, the workers used a method known as a *La trace* and the reader should also try that way of working the cordonnette. The instructions will be found on p. 70.

The way described here is the lazy one by couching the outline of a flower on to a piece of prepared backing material. Place the couching stitches very close together. This is only for practice and will not be removed from the backing when finished as it is only an outline.

Thread the needle with whatever thread would be used for the size of flower being worked and run the needle through three or four couch stitches down to the base of the petal; pull the thread through till the end is just caught under the first couch stitch it went through. Make a knot stitch.

Fig. 24a The buttonhole stitches can be turned at the end of each thick line

Fig. 24b The outline of a flower, each petal to be worked following the instructions

A partially worked Point de Venise bag by Catherine Barley, giving details of the couronnes and picots. The raised cordonnette has 64 laid threads of 20 crochet cotton at the highest points

To start the raising
Take a thread and fold in half (this is the cordonnette); take the needle through the fold, and then work five or six buttonhole stitches over the couched thread (the cordonnet) and over the laid thread of the cordonnette.

For the first increase
Fold the ends of the cordonnette back on themselves, leaving the ends lying beyond the buttonhole stitches just made, then work another half a dozen stitches over the cordonnette, the original laid threads and the fresh

The finished Point de Venise bag, worked in 80/3s ecru silks, attached on to a cream silk foundation

pair. At the loop where the threads were folded back on themselves, pull just one, then the other, until the ends of the threads are just under the first of the stitches. Work another few stitches before making the next increase.

For the second increase

Take a fresh thread, fold in half and lay the ends of these new threads over the last stitches made, make six or more stitches over all threads then carefully pull the ends through until they just disappear under the stitches. This gives six cordonnette threads. Work six more stitches.

For the third increase

Take another two pieces of thread, fold in half making four ends of the cordonnette, lay over the six stitches just worked and make another six stitches over all threads. Pull through as before to loose the ends. Work over these ten threads round the top of the petal.

To start the decreasing

Coming down the other side of the petal first, when the point opposite the last increase is reached, shear off four threads as close as possible to the buttonhole stitches. Make sure you keep the working thread clear of the scissors. Work 12 stitches and cut off another two threads, then continue in this way to the base of the flower shape, ending with two threads.

Laying the threads

Working a piece of lace would need the same forward planning as shown when laying the cordonnet. For instance, if working a complete flower, work up one side of the first petal, over the top and down to the point where the next petal joins the first. Take one thread and the working thread down to the centre of the flower. With the working thread make a knot stitch to hold the cordonnette thread in position at the centre of the flower. Fold the cordonnette over on to itself, then buttonhole over the original thread (cordonnet), over the doubled thread of the cordonnette and over the working thread that was taken down to the centre. Work about six stitches, then bring another thread down from where they are hanging at the end of the petal just worked. Fold the new thread over as before, then work over all the threads until reaching the join.

It is important that the needle is taken through the last made buttonhole stitch of the previous petal, before working up and over the top of the next petal. Use all the threads from the first petal and those that have been worked up from the centre. It will soon be obvious that by working the buttonhole stitches through the top of those made at the join of the petals, the second petal can be made to look as if it lies on top of the first. This can be seen in the photograph on p. 52.

A Point de Venise wall hanging worked by Catherine Barley in dusty pinks and ecru-coloured silks, showing some of the threads used in raising. 20 crochet cotton and 130/3s silk were used for the raising and as many as 30 threads. The fillings used are corded stitch, Gros Point Diamonds and Pea stitch variation, with veins of Alençon beads dividing the leaves. The Gros Point de Venise stitches also used can be found in *The Technique of Needlepoint Lace*

50

The finished Point de Venise wall hanging

Just before reaching the end of a run, cut off most of the threads, leaving two or three, then work two stitches and cut away leaving one thread. Force the last two stitches into the space left and cut off. It may be necessary to thread up a small needle with the working thread to get through the buttonhole stitches to fasten off.

If at any point during cutting off the cordonnette threads the working thread is cut, and it does happen, unpick one or two stitches and tuck the end of the unpicked thread behind the rest of the cordonnette. Start with a new working thread and run the needle through one or two couched stitches ahead of where the thread was cut. Take the new thread up and through the loop of the last stitch, keeping the thumb on the end of the new thread to stop it pulling

through, and work two or three stitches. These stitches would be worked over the end of the cut thread, the new working thread and the cordonnette and the join will neither show nor come apart. One or even two extra threads in the cordonnette at any one time does not show a marked difference in the size of the edging; if a thread needs to be cut out to reduce the number, always cut away the shortest one.

Turning the edges
The cordonnette can be made to appear to twist and curve around the edge of the petals or borders. Practise along the edge of a petal laid as suggested at the beginning of this chapter. Work over the cordonnette to the point where the single line becomes two (*see Fig. 49*), keeping the knot of the stitch to the outside of the petal. Take the needle under the cordonnette and give a slight pull on the thread. Turn the work upside down and the knot of the stitch

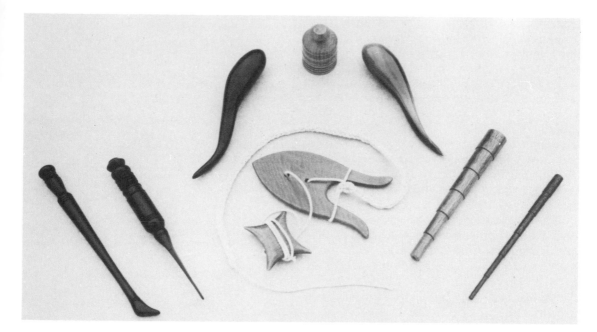

will now be facing the inside of the petal. Work along the inner line to the point where it becomes a single line again. Take the needle under the cordonnette as before, turn the work back to its original position. Give a slight pull on the working thread to make the stitches start to turn over, then continue down to the base of the petal with the knot of the stitch now on the outside of the petal. The outside top line of the petal would be whipped over, the start and finish of the thread being taken through the buttonhole stitches already worked.

Any part of a design can be treated in this way. The knot of the stitch can be made to stay upright if the thread is pulled through and up when working the stitch, and this can be followed through by turning the work upside down and continuing to buttonhole in the same direction. The needle can then be taken back under the cordonnette, giving the thread a slight pull and, with the work turned back, the rest of the cordonnette can be laid giving the impression that the whole edge has turned over.

COURONNES

Couronnes were a feature of Venetian Raised Point lace, and are the final decoration added after the work has been removed from the backing material. Couronnes are scrolls and rings which are made separately and attached to the lace with small stab stitches, usually at the centres of flowers or at the base of a design where a number of different fillings meet. They are often ornamented with picots and several can be added on top of each other to give the finished lace the appearance of sculpture.

The ring stick

A variety of different size knitting needles or fine dowling can be used to form the rings, but an accurately made ring stick that has proportional dimensions along its length, ranging from a small diameter at the top to a large ring at the bottom is much more convenient to carry around. The ring stick is an important part of the equipment needed by a needlepoint lace worker and all types of couronnes are made with it. The more highly polished the stick the easier it is to remove the wound thread, so never allow the stick to become greasy or sticky from hot hands. Never put wood directly in water as all the little hairs or fibres in the wood lift; just wipe with a damp cloth and rub over with a white furniture polish afterwards.

To find the size of ring needed, lay the stick over the hole that the ring is to cover allowing for the turns of thread; the sides of the hole should be just visible to allow for the thickness of the buttonhole stitches. It is a good idea to make one or two rings over the same diameter of the stick using different numbers of turns round the ring to get an idea as to the size that part of the stick makes.

If a ring turns out to be too small or too big, keep it for another time. A little box of discarded rings is worth its weight in gold when confronted with a pattern needing dozens of rings. A ring that turns out too small can have a number of scallops worked round the outside which will bring it up to size.

To work a couronne

Take a long length of thread and wrap the end around the end of the ring stick a number of times, at the desired diameter. The greater the number of rounds, the thicker the finished ring. Slip the needle under all the threads while still on the stick and make the first buttonhole stitch. Once this first stitch is made, gently force the wrapping threads down the stick but, before taking off the very end, hold between finger and thumb and make some more buttonhole stitches.

It is often easier to work away from you, that is, putting the needle into the loop and forming the buttonhole stitch on the outside. You will find that half-way around the ring the stitches can be pushed closer together to make sure the stitches are really well packed in. When the threads are all covered, take the needle through the buttonhole stitch first made, along at the

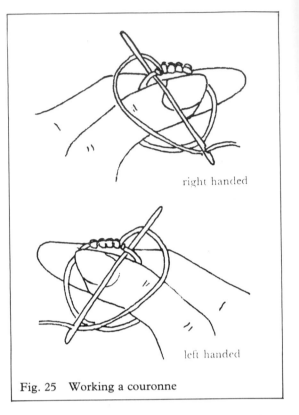

right handed

left handed

Fig. 25 Working a couronne

back of the ring. Make a note at this stage of the size of the ring used to wrap the threads around, how many times the thread was wrapped around the ring stick, just how many stitches were needed to fill the ring and the size of thread used. It all proves very useful information later.

Not all couronnes are made on a ring stick; they can be formed directly on to the cordonnet. Venetian laces from the early sixteenth century show the use of the added refinement of scallops worked into the laid threads. The scallops were worked in double and treble layers with picots along the entire length.

5.
Designing

Lace is soft and dainty, especially when used for articles of clothing, children's wear, bridal veils or bouquets. So, a soft flowing design is in keeping in this context. The original designs in the fifteenth century were square or rectangular and, until the time the cordonnet was laid independently of any material base, they were worked in long lengths along the weft or warp of the material. The designs then became curved and rounded, one motif trailing into another. The designers took their ideas from the plants available at the time. One plant in particular seems to have been a favourite both with the lace and crewel-work designers. This was the acanthus, which was introduced into Britain in the early thirteenth century and, by the fifteenth century, was a well-known plant on most country estates.

The motif which characterises the Corinthian capital is derived from the foliage of either *Acanthus mollis* or the Spiney Leaved Bear's Breeches. So the leaf was the inspiration for designers for many centuries before lace was in vogue. Having stood the test of time, there must be something worth preserving, so the next few motifs will be based on the leaf of this plant. Many designs are so stylised that any resemblance to the real thing is far removed. But, as the leaf begins to wilt, the points along the edges curl over and the centre of the leaf turns round clockwise, and it is in this condition that the resemblance to the designs can be seen, not the design resembling the full leaf.

Usually the motifs are connected by scrolls which, for the most part, are based on an S bend. Flower arrangers will be familiar with the Hogarth bend which is an elongated S. Even if drawing is not a strong point with the reader, playing with this shape produces some very unexpected designs. A mirror image can put another dimension to the original shape and, when laid in different positions or an extra line is added, the design alters completely. This information is much the same as that given in *The Technique of Needlepoint Lace*, but I make no apology for repeating it here as it is a very good starting point.

Do not be content with the first S, the more it is drawn the better the flow of the line. When satisfied with the design add another line along the outside edge. Mirror image the complete drawing by holding the first sheet of paper against a window, putting another sheet of paper over the first, and make a copy of it; use carbon paper if it is available. Turn the second paper over and trace the drawing just made, thus giving the mirror image of the first drawing. The two drawings can be laid side by side in many different directions until a pleasing design is found. The scrolls added to the stylised leaf will make a repeat pattern which will, in turn, make a design.

When forming a design, remember that the solid parts worked in corded stitch are going to stand out against a background of open-work stitches. Even so, do not use the corded stitch only as this will give the effect of a mass of heavy design. Instead, lighten the effect with the more open-work stitches; this will give shades of light. When working a leaf, for instance, if one side of the centre vein is worked in corded stitch and the other side in close buttonhole stitch one side will appear lighter than the other.

There are many readers who will be inclined to give up when confronted with the prospect of having to draw their own design. So here are a few ways of 'cheating' which still enable you to come up with something different. Coats Publications issue a craft folio called 'Beautiful Butterflies' No. 013. The designs given are for

Fig. 26   A design for a lampshade by Mary
Anderson, taking motifs from Deighton transfers

embroidery, but those same designs worked in
needlepoint lace take on a different aspect. The
finished lace can still be used as the folio
suggests but it will be a design worked in a
completely different way. This is not the only
folio produced by Coats, but it is one that a
student has previously worked from, and is
shown in *Creative Design in Needlepoint Lace*.

A delightful way of getting something really
special, without the headache of designing it
yourself, is to send for the catalogue from
Deighton Bros Ltd of their wide range of
transfers. The address is given in the List of
Suppliers. There are edgings as well as circles,
squares, and triangles. These can be mirror-
imaged and backed together to use for veils or
underwear. Most drawing office suppliers have
an instant print service that can reduce the
design down to the size required. Many of the
transfers are already printed in a number of

different sizes, especially the ecclesiastical designs. Most of these can be adapted and used
for needlepoint lace. After all, it was in the
convents that the beginnings of this type of lace
were first worked and where a lot of the best
work was executed. The Jacobean designs are
typical foliate acanthus leaves and the stylised
flowers are of the type used in the lace for the
Gros Point de Venise right through the centuries to the Point de Gaze of the nineteenth and
twentieth centuries. The cutwork transfers are
also typical of the tape lace that was fashionable
just before the First World War. The transfers
can be used to make a design to fit any given
shape. Choose one or two of the Jacobean
flowers, draw or trace off the same number of
mirror images and arrange within the area
needed, infilling if necessary with a leaf or
scroll. Each of the following designs are iso-
lated motifs, taken at random from Deighton
transfers and laid to form a square. These three

Fig. 27 Another design composed of motifs from
Deighton transfer

designs will be carried through all stages to form projects.

PROJECT 1

Motif 1 was taken from transfer No. Q3324 and drawn on to tracing paper. Take a square of tracing paper and fold, first in half then in quarters. Then fold from the centre to the extreme corners forming a triangle. Make sure the creases are distinct and visible when the paper is unfolded. Draw a pencil line through the centre of the traced flower from the tip of the top petal down through the centre to between the two bottom petals. Place the single flower under the square of tracing paper making the pencil line lie directly under the crease running from the centre out to the middle of one side. The points of the two bottom petals should be touching the creases running from the centre to the corners of the square. Fold the paper across its half-way mark and trace the flower off on to the other side. Open the paper and lay the flower motif under to trace off the third side, making sure that the tips of the bottom petals touch the bottom petals already drawn. Then fold in half and draw off the last flower.

Fig. 28(2) shows the little scroll needed to connect the flowers together at the top. The area enclosed by this little scroll is called a casket and is always filled with an open-work stitch. Use the directions for working pin stitch (*see p. 21*) to attach the linen to the centre of the mat.

The sampler was worked in 40 crochet thread (Coats) which is right for this size motif. Staying with this size thread choose an open-work stitch for the casket and work the little scroll in close buttonhole stitch.

Laying the cordonnette

When working the cordonnette, finish off each of the scrolls laying the 40 crochet thread for the laid thread and using 80 crochet thread to buttonhole over it. Place the stitches close together, but do not crowd them or the edging will pucker.

Start the cordonnette at the centre of the bottom petal and work round to where the second petal starts. Take one thread from the cordonnette and the working thread to the centre ring. Fasten with a knot stitch, buttonhole stitch from the centre ring over the two threads back to the rest of the laid threads, then work all threads to continue round the next outside petal in a similar fashion. Finish off all outside petals, then start with fresh threads to work the two middle petals. The centre of the flower can either be finished off with a laid cordonnette or a separate couronne can be worked and attached when the mat is removed from the backing.

PROJECT 2

Motif 3 was laid differently for drawing up. Make the separate drawing of both 3 and 4. Then fold the square of tracing paper in the same way as given for motif 1. Draw a line through the centre of the bell shape, but this time lay the pencil line under the fold that runs from the centre of the square to one of the four outside corners. Fold the tracing paper into a triangle and trace the second bell shape. The separate paper is now laid under the square to trace off the third bell, making sure the tips of the outside petals are touching the petals already drawn. Then fold the paper into the second triangle to trace off the fourth bell shape.

Motif 4 is now placed under the tracing paper and manoeuvred into position to reach from the centre bottom of one bell to its neighbour, before being traced off. The tracing paper can be folded as before to find the position for the other three scrolls.

PROJECT 3

Because motifs No 5 and 6 are on a smaller scale they were laid differently for tracing off. Draw the first motif, then turn it over and trace off a mirror image. Fold the paper square in the same way as before, but this time the two motifs take up the area between two half folds. The quarter fold that runs from the centre of the square to the outside edge at the corner comes through the centre between a motif and its mirror image.

The dimensions are the same size as the first mat using motifs 1 and 2. Because the size of

Fig. 28 The motifs for the three projects

these motifs is reduced they should be worked in finer threads. The actual motif and scroll can be worked in 80 crochet cotton, while the casket would look better worked in the 100 Crochet cotton. These threads in the same sizes, but in silk, can be purchased from Leonie Cox (*see p. 117*).

Another way of working this mat would be to work the motif and scroll in corded stitch leaving the centre empty. Then appliqué the finished ring on to net. The centre of the mat, the centres of the flowers and the casket could then be filled in with needlerun stitches. These will be found on pp. 115–123 of *The Technique of Needlepoint Lace,* under the section on Limerick Lace.

Fig. 29   Motifs 1 and 2 laid to the folds in the paper

The first motif, showing the couching in progress

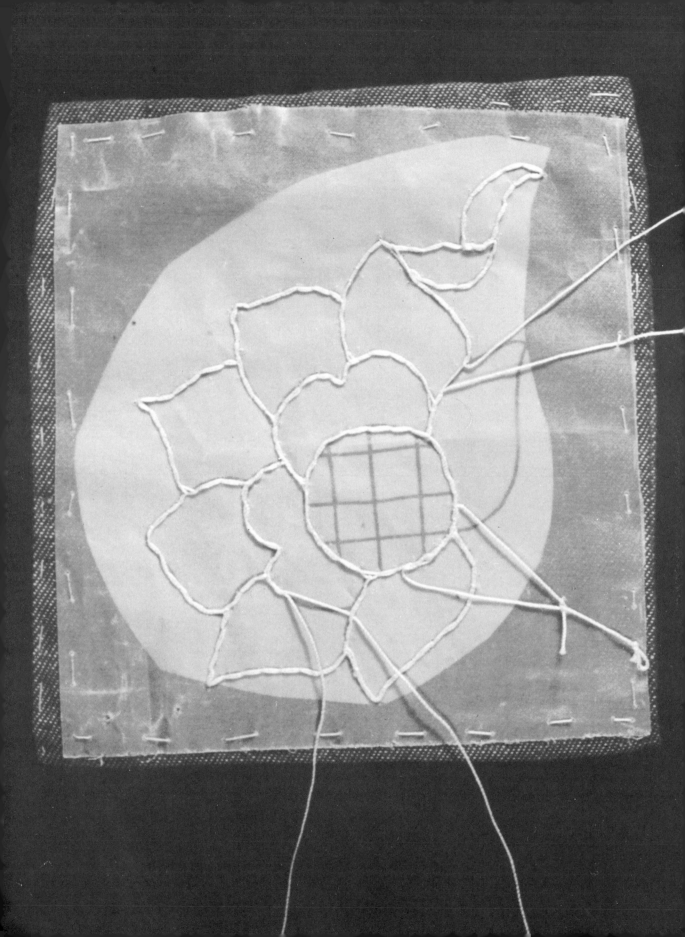

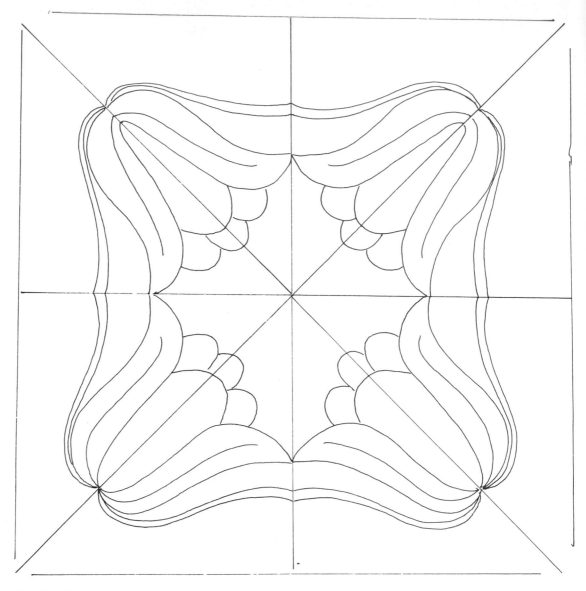

Fig. 30   Motifs 3 and 4; the tips of the outside
petals should touch the lines of the centre fold.
Lay motif 4 last

Motifs 3 and 4 shown here worked in a variety of
stitches by Pat Gibson

62

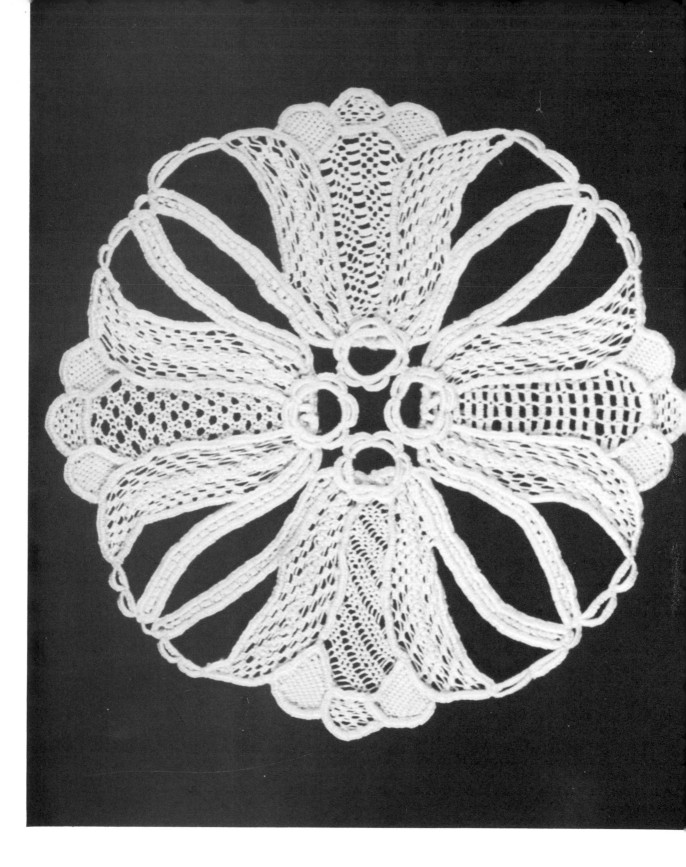

Fig. 31   Motifs 5 and 6; the two motifs take up
the area between two half-folds

Motifs 1 and 2 finished and arranged on a pattern

A collar worked by Elizabeth (Jetlag) Landry – her
first piece – worked in antique thread which was
originally obtained from Hilatura Coats of
Barcelona, Spain. The collar is a good example of
the method of designing described in this chaper

6.
Edgings and Patterns

The following three edgings are taken from pieces of sixteenth-century Venetian lace known as *Punto Tagliato Fogliami*. This was the early Gros Point de Venise. Although given here as the first patterns because of their simplicity, the edgings formed only a small part of the most exquisite lace. The stitches were worked round the outside edge of the lace and were also used to edge the Couronnes, with the working thread so fine it can scarcely be seen without magnification. A loop often had a picot placed between each stitch and, in some cases, the picot on the top loop would have three picots worked into it. The needles used 400 years ago were incredibly fine; in spite of modern technology, the finest needles readily available today are in the region of size 10 and it would be impossible to emulate the early Venetian work using them. The ultra fine thread was equivalent to a 350/2s and was made from pure flax. The finest thread available to us is ultra fine silk or the Honiton lace cotton. These are still twice as thick as the original, but do allow for some extra fine lace to be worked.

EDGING 1

These instructions are for a very simple edging that could be used to decorate babies' dresses or could make an 'off the peg' blouse into something quite different. Just edging the top and bottom of the cuffs, the edge of the collar and both sides of the buttonhole band down the

front of the blouse, can put it into quite a different class. It is quick and easy to work but looks most effective.

General hints

When working this edging it would be advisable to practise the stitch round a handkerchief first. Any variation in the size of the loops would not show up in the same way as it would down the front of a blouse. Before working, the handkerchief should be tacked to a piece of backing material as shown in the photograph. This will keep the work from puckering up.

Make a point of working to the end of a loop before having to start a new thread. Run the old thread through the hem for about 1·25 cm ($\frac{1}{2}$ in) then cut off. The new thread is taken through the hem from the opposite direction to the old thread, and the needle is brought out at the base of the last loop worked then the pattern continued.

Working instructions

Make a knot in the end of the working thread and run through the hem of the handkerchief, as already described, and bring the thread out at A. Take the needle through a small amount of material at B. Then back again to A, and pick up the material as before.

Buttonhole over the threads just made, working an even number of stitches as far as B. After the first loop has been buttonholed over, cut off the knot.

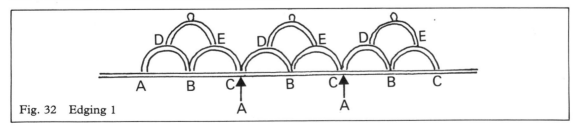

Fig. 32   Edging 1

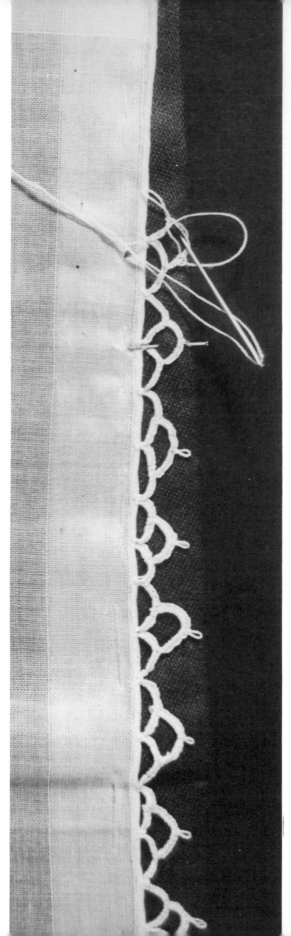

Take the thread over to point C, then back to B. Take the needle through the top of the last buttonhole stitch of the first loop. Buttonhole stitch back over these last laid threads, working half the number of stitches made on the first loop, which will take the worker to the centre of the second loop.

Now take the needle over and through the centre of the two stitches in the middle of the first loop at D. Go back to the centre top of the second loop, take the needle through the top of the last stitch made at this point, then back through the top of the first loop as before at D.

There will be three threads lying between the two base loops and the worker will be at the point marked D. Work half the number of stitches on this loop that have been worked on the first base loop, make a picot as shown in the diagram and work the other half of the stitches. This finishes the top loop and the worker is at the centre of the second base loop. Take the needle through the top of the last stitch made on the second loop and work the required number of stitches to finish the second loop.

These three loops form the pattern and are repeated for the length required. Keep the same number of stitches in each loop and remember the picot in the centre of each top loop.

Güterman sewing silk 100/3, which is available in a large range of colours, is an easy thread to work with for this pattern.

EDGING 2

This can be found in early *Punto in Aria* as part of a larger edging, placed round the outside of the Vandyke points.

Working instructions

The instructions follow the first few moves of the previous pattern. Join in the thread by running the needle through the hem for a short distance then bring the needle out at A.

Insert again at B picking up a small amount of material, then back to A and buttonhole over the two threads as far as B.

The first edging being worked directly on to a handkerchief

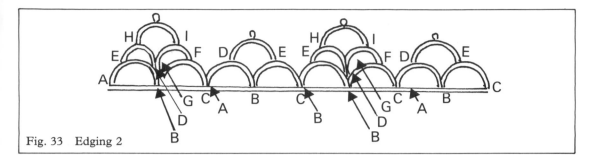

Fig. 33   Edging 2

Take the needle through at C then back to B.

Take the needle through the last buttonhole stitch of the first loop in the pattern at B. Work half the number of stitches made on the first loop to bring the worker to the point marked F.

Then take the needle through the top of the stitch directly between two loops at D, pick up the top of the centre stitch, and then over to E.

Take the needle through the top of the centre stitch of the first loop at E and retrace the thread just laid from E to D to F, and return in the same way to E. There will now be three threads waiting to be buttonholed over.

Work from E to G, then take the needle down to D.

Pick up the top of the last stitch worked at G and work over the three threads to I.

Now take the needle back and through the top of the centre stitch at H and back to I then back to H. Buttonhole to the centre of this top loop, make a picot and buttonhole over to I; this will finish the top loop of the pattern.

Take the needle through the top of the last stitch on the middle row at I and work down to F. Again go through the top of the last stitch of the bottom row at F and work down to C.

For the next set of loops, C beomes A and these loops are worked in the same way as the instructions given in the first pattern. C becomes A to start the three-loop block each time.

The two previous edgings are small enough to be worked directly on to the garment or into the border of a handkerchief. This being so, threads can be run through the hem to start and finish. Always start a new thread at the base of a loop and finish in the same way.

The following edging is too wide to work in this way and will need two rows of couched threads A-B to form the base. These two threads are then used as a cordonnet and all loops are worked from them.

EDGING 3

This is much more elaborate and needs some forward planning; it is also best to couch some of the threads before commencing the main piece.

Preparing the pattern

First of all, draw off or trace the number of repeats needed; each repeat illustrated equals 5·08 cm (2 in) but the design can be enlarged or reduced according to the size required. If a corner is needed the design can be turned at a 90° angle and the space between the two end motifs filled in. The individual raised loop

Fig. 34   Repeat motifs for the third edging

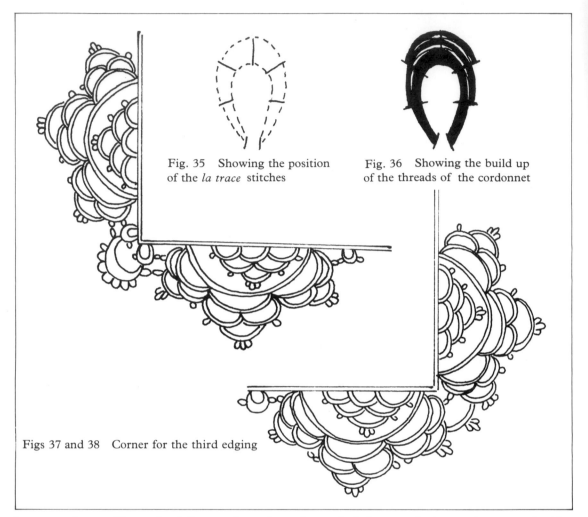

Fig. 35   Showing the position of the *la trace* stitches

Fig. 36   Showing the build up of the threads of the cordonnet

Figs 37 and 38   Corner for the third edging

between the motifs can be left out altogether and the corner bridged by a loop with picots. If extra space has to be filled in, end and start the two sides with a raised loop and place a large raised loop with a series of picots to bridge over from one motif to the other above the smaller two loops (*see Figs 37–38*).

Once the length of the repeats has been drawn up, cover with acetate film and attach to the backing material. The raised loops between the motifs must have seven stitches placed as shown on the pattern (*see Fig. 37*), two small ones at the bottom, two slightly larger each side and one even larger at the top. When the pattern is prepared in this way it is called *la trace*. The cordonnet is then run through these stitches until packed quite solid and this is then buttonholed over, placing a picot at each side. Having determined how many buttonhole stitches are required to reach the position of the first picot, work out from that calculation how many will be needed to reach the other picot, leaving enough room to work the same number of stitches from the second picot down to the base as was used from the base up to the first picot at the beginning; run the needle through the cordonnet to fasten off. With a design of this size, new threads have to be run in and out in the pattern itself because a sufficently long thread would be unmanageable. To finish off a thread at any point in the design, reach the end of a loop, lay the remaining thread over the next loop and take it out through the backing material. The new thread is taken through from the back of the backing material and laid beside the old thread over the loop. Take the needle through the last stitch made and work at least four stitches over the original and the two extra threads. Both the end of the old thread and the beginning of the new thread can then be cut off before continuing working over the loop.

Never cut threads off at a picot; always work at least two stitches beyond it, as a picot is a weak spot and needs the buttonhole stitches placed tightly to hold it in place.

Because the pattern can be used on a larger or smaller scale, it is difficult to give set numbers of stitches needed to fill each loop but once the first repeat is worked, make a note of the stitches placed before and after each picot. Make a point of working one stitch between each of the picots in the groups of three on the top loops of each motif. The *trace* should be drawn off on to tracing paper and laid over the pattern, in order to show the points that should be given a couched stitch, to keep the scallops in position while being worked. It is only necesssary to lay this tracing over the top of the acetate film as a guide line, not to have it permanently under the film, and once the placing of the stitches for the first motif has been laid it will be easy enough to follow through with the rest of the pattern.

To work the loops between the motifs
Work the little raised loops between the motifs first. The seven stitches of the *trace* having been laid in, take the needle through all the stitches of the *trace*, leaving a tail which can be cut off once the buttonhole stitches have been started. Bring the needle out of and over the last of the *trace* stitches then back under the others to the starting point. Do this until the bottom *trace* stitches cannot hold any more thread, then use the next two *trace* stitches up on each side and come out of, over and back through these five *trace* stitches until these too are filled. Then continue working through the top three *trace* stitches. Take the thread through the backing material and cut off.

Now buttonhole closely over all laid threads up to the picot mark. Form the picot and work over the extra threads. Allow these threads to lie flat and do not work the buttonhole stitches

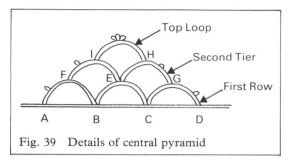

Fig. 39 Details of central pyramid

tight, otherwise the threads of the cordonnet will bunch up and lie one on top of the other instead of being allowed to make the shape. Work the buttonhole stitches close together, which is different from working tight stitches. Then continue down the other side, forming the second picot in its due place. Fasten off by running the thread back through four or five stitches.

The central pyramid of loops is worked next and it is a good idea at this point to draw up a separate motif on a larger scale and note down the number of stitches used at each section of the work so that the following repeats receive the correct number of stitches at the same points.

To work the central pyramid
Run the working thread through the two couched threads at the base to point A, make a knot stitch over the two threads ready to make the first loop. Take the thread over to B and make a knot stitch; then to C and again knot; lastly across to D and knot.

Retrace, taking the needle through the knot stitch at each point, keeping each loop the same height and ending back at A with two threads to each loop. Buttonhole over the two threads to a point halfway between A and F and make a picot. Then continue to buttonhole over the loop to B.

Take the needle through the knot stitch and buttonhole on over to the point marked E. Take the thread over to F and through the top of the middle stitch of this first loop, back to E and go through the top of the last stitch worked at E then back to F. Buttonhole over the three threads just laid and make a picot halfway between F and I.

Continue over the loop to E and halfway

71

A corner worked around a handkerchief by Pat
Gibson using the third edging

over the second loop to H. Take the needle
through the top of the centre stitch at I, back to
H and through the top of the last stitch made at
this point. Now take the thread back through
the top of the same stitch at I, then commence
to buttonhole over this top loop, placing three
picots in the centre with one buttonhole stitch
between each picot; continue down to H.

Take the needle through the top of the last
stitch at H and on down this loop to G, placing

a picot at the halfway mark. Pick up the top of
the last stitch made at G and work down to D
with the last picot made halfway betwen G and
D.

Make a knot stitch into the two couched base
threads and run the needle through two or
three couched stitches before cutting off.

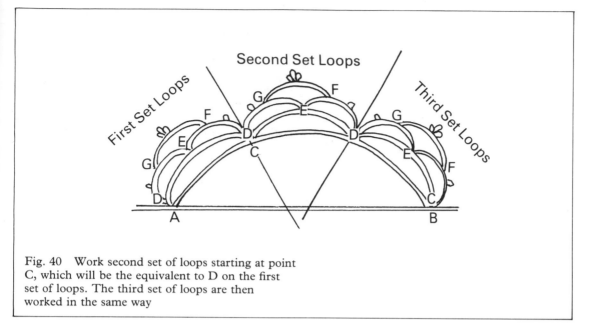

Fig. 40 Work second set of loops starting at point C, which will be the equivalent to D on the first set of loops. The third set of loops are then worked in the same way

To work the outside edge

Now draw an enlarged version of the outside edge to be numbered up in the same way as the central pyramid. Put the *trace* stitches into position; even if it was found possible to work the centre without the help of the *trace*, it is advised that it is used for the outside edge.

To start the design, run the thread through the cordonnet and make a knot stitch at A. Take the needle through the *trace* stitches from A to B, make a knot stitch at B and back through the trace to A. Take the needle through the knot stitch at A. Repeat this movement making four laid threads. Buttonhole over these four laid threads as far as C.

Take the thread back to form a loop (second row) taking the needle through the top of the stitch at A, then back to C through the top of the stitch as before and back to A. Buttonhole the whole length of this loop.

Take the needle through at E and then over to D forming the two loops of the third row. Retrace back to E and on to C and back again.

Make use of the *trace* stitches to hold the loops in shape.

Over the three threads, buttonhole from D to E making a picot halfway between D and G and then on to F. Take the needle back to G through the top of the centre stitch and back to

F through the top of the stitch then back to G. Buttonhole over these three laid threads till reaching nearly to centre top. Make three picots with one buttonhole stitch between each, then buttonhole down to F.

Take the needle through the top of the last stitch made on the third row at F and then buttonhole down to C, making a picot at the half-way mark.

C now becomes A to start the next scallop.

After the first few samplers have been worked, most students are impatient to start on something simple. A collar is often chosen for the first big project because it can be worn and is there as proof of the student's capabilities.

COLLAR 1

This particular design is very straightforward.

Materials
Large sheet of brown paper
Large sheet of drawing paper
Large sheet of tracing paper
Acetate film or drawing office linen
Backing material
Threads equivalent to 60 crochet cotton for the

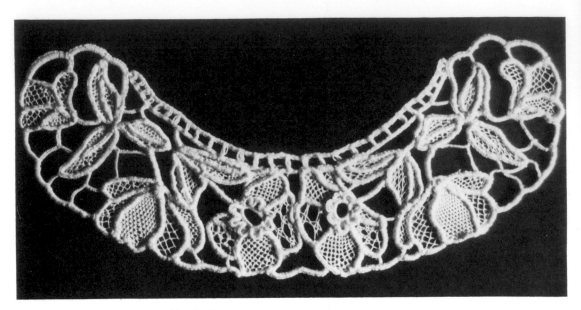

Half a Peter Pan collar worked by Janie
Dobrick – her first piece

Fig. 41   Collar 1: worked this size it fits the large
doll. It can be reduced further for the smaller dolls

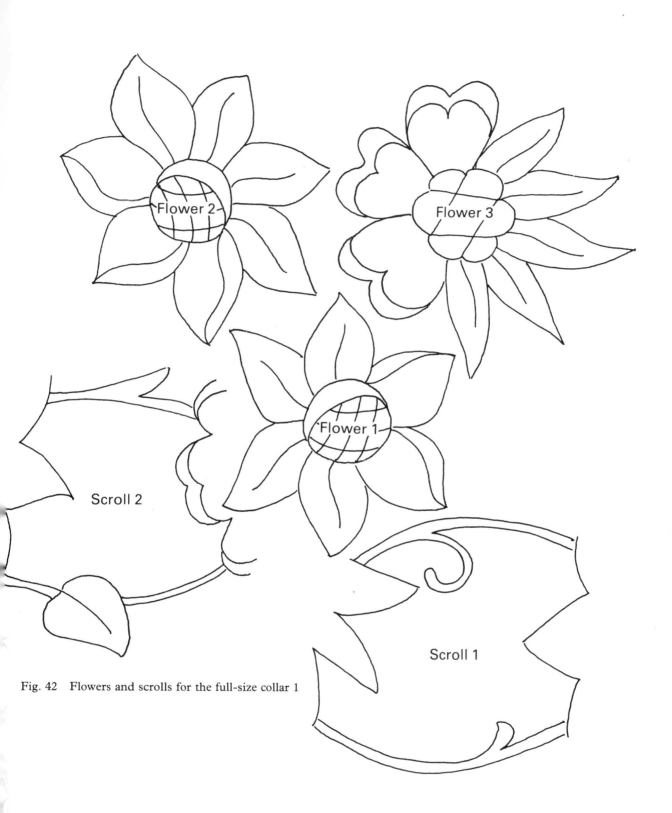

Fig. 42   Flowers and scrolls for the full-size collar 1

cordonnet, machine sewing cotton for couching the cordonnet, the equivalent to 80 crochet cotton for working the flowers and 100 thread for the caskets. If using silks, 80/3s and 100/3s for the collar and 60/3s for the cordonnet. If the small scale collar is being worked for a doll 100/3s and 130/3s will be needed.

Preparing the pattern

The whole collar can be worked straight from the design, there is no need to work each flower separately.

The design is shown quarter size to fit a 60 cm (24 in) doll (*see p. 74*) but it is easy to enlarge by the method given on pp. 80–81. To help the reader even further all the motifs and the caskets have been drawn full size and can be used in the following way. Study the layout of the design and trace off on to separate tracing paper four tracings of flower 3, two tracings of flower 2 and one of flower 1.

Enlarge the neckband to fit the dress it will be worn with and cut a curved band in drawing paper. Take a large piece of thick brown wrapping paper slightly bigger than the overall collar pattern. Then cut a piece of tracing paper to the same size and stick both papers together at the four corners with transparent adhesive tape.

Lay the papers on a flat surface and push the cut band of the neckline between the two papers centre top. Now position the seven flowers following the design given in the book.

Place flower 1 centre back between the two papers, with the two petals touching the neckbands, as shown in the completed collar drawing. Then roughly position the other flowers.

The scrolls now have to be drawn and mirror imaged as shown on p. 64; scroll 1 has to be drawn twice with two mirror images drawn while scroll 2 only has to be mirror-imaged once. Place into position between the flowers; the petals of the flowers should lie over the drawing shown at the end of each scroll.

When all the design is in position under the tracing paper any final adjustment to any of the designs should be done with a knitting needle, as putting the hand between the sheets of paper often moves the motifs that are already in the right place.

Placing the hand on the top of the tracing paper to hold everything in place, trace off the design with a nylon tip rolla-ball pen.

This completed collar drawing should now be covered with film, mounted on to backing material and the caskets should have the cordonnet couched completely round each and the fillings worked. Each casket can be worked in the same filling or two fillings can be worked in alternate spaces.

Working instructions

The flowers are easier to work if each one is mounted up individually and worked completely, apart from the final cordonnette. When the flowers are finished they are removed from their backing, cleaned of threads, laid in place on the complete collar, and sewn to the cordonnet threads at the ends of each casket.

The flowers need to be solid so that they stand out from the caskets. Choose any of the corded stitches for every other petal. Those remaining can be worked in double or treble Bruxelles stitch or the pea stitch variations. Limit the number of stitch patterns used in the flowers to three or four or they will look fussy.

The cordonnette should be worked round the caskets first then, when laid round the flowers, work over the last stitch or two at the end of each casket. This will make the flowers appear to be lying over the cordonnette of the casket instead of being on the same level as them. Do make sure that the laid cordonnet at the end of each casket, which is part of the adjoining flower, is picked up in the top cordonnette as it is worked, or there will be a loose thread floating at the back of the collar when it is removed from the backing material.

Use at least six strands of 60 thread round all outside edges; many more can be used to give a sculptured effect. It is best to raise one side of each petal higher than its neighbour or to enlarge the cordonnet, then add where needed when the pattern calls for wider areas (*see p. 48*).

The centres of the flowers can be filled with a woven wheel or any of the fillings using a square mesh, the directions for which will be found in *Creative Design in Needlepoint Lace,* p. 105.

Fig. 43 The complete collar 2—one-quarter full size, to fit 24 in doll

Fig. 44 Centre back of full-size collar 2

Fig. 45a   First section, to follow on from centre back

Fig. 45b   Second section left

Fig. 45c   Bottom section, left front

Fig. 45   Mirror image these three sections to follow off from centre for right-hand side of collar

COLLAR 2

This is a much more advanced design using 100/3s and 130/3s silk thread. Use has been made of rings, couronnes, scalloped edges and woven wheels, but is still within the scope of a newcomer to needlepoint lace. The complete design is shown to the size needed for a 60 cm (24 in) doll (*see p. 77*) and, if working to this scale, keep all stitches to Bruxelles and corded. Couronnes can be worked round the stem on the back section and small rings worked over a size 12 knitting needle will be sufficient for the other circles; to enlarge the rings, wrap more threads round the needle before buttonholing. The motifs have been drawn up to full scale and the collar can be laid and drawn by the same method as for collar 1.

Each of the sections can be worked separately then relaid and stitched to the completed collar design before laying the final cordon-

The back of the pattern for the second collar, being worked by the author in 100 silks

nette. The back panel has been worked to give some idea of the stitches that can be used and the same stitches can be continued to each end. The first edging has been worked as a couronne round the centre petal of the sprays each side of the central motif at the back. The central motif has a woven wheel in the middle. The cordonnette is composed of between six and ten threads of 100/3 thread.

The number of different stitches used is entirely up to the worker and the same ones as used in the first collar would be perfectly acceptable. The laid cordonnette holds all the separate pieces together, but a few extra stitches oversewing the ends of the pieces at the joins before the cordonnette is laid would strengthen the collar considerably.

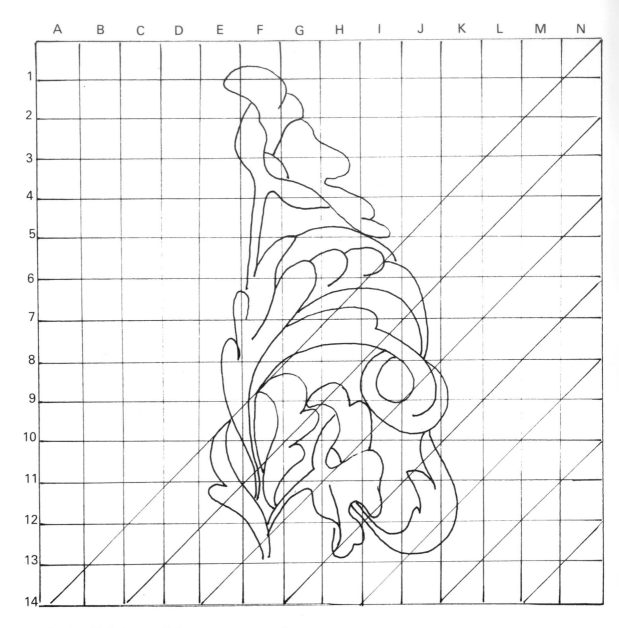

Fig. 46   Full-size motif drawn on square grid

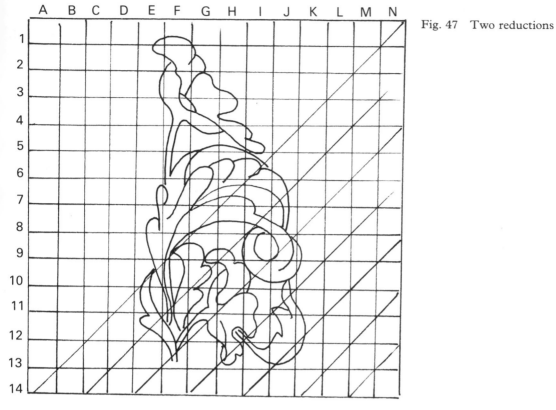

Fig. 47   Two reductions

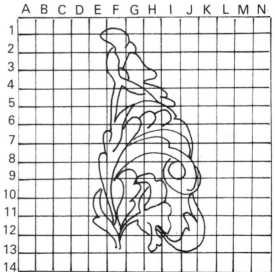

Fig. 48   Four reductions; the diagonal line is not necessary on such a small reduction as this

THE BRIDAL OUTFIT

The following designs are intended for a bridal outfit but would look just as effective worked in colours for evening wear. They were designed by Shirley Warren, a student who first came to my classes two years ago, never having done needlepoint lace before. Although the designs appear complicated at first, a closer look proves otherwise, the whole collection being a good object lesson in relating items within a group or set.

First, the same motifs have been used throughout to build up quite different shapes without losing any of the first impact. Study the coronet and the shoe front. The shapes within the design are identical so, with a soft pencil, black out the background behind the coronet, in the same way as the shoe, to bring the design to the foreground. This particular shape can be used in two ways. With the straight edge along the bottom and the finished work starched, it would stand erect for a head-dress; it should be worked in white silk for the bride and in colours to match the flowers or outfits of the bridesmaids. Turned the other way up it would be worked in silk, using deep jewel colours across the waistline for the belt of an evening dress. Worked with subtle colours in 80 thread it could be applied to a soft kid belt to wear with a wool dress or suit.

The caps of the sleeves were intended for a bride's dress, but worked in coloured threads the design would be appropriate for an evening gown. The square neckline and shoulder straps would look right for either a sundress or a nightdress. The former would be best in 80 crochet cotton with a raised cordonnette to give a crisp clear line, while a nightdress top would need 130/3s silk, which is a very fine thread, to give a soft feel to the garment and with a plain buttonholed edge instead of a cordonnette.

Whichever pattern is being worked, make sure that the size is right before proceeding. Often a design can be lengthened or shortened by adding or taking away a scroll or leaf; if

Fig. 49 With the straight edge as the base, this design could be used as a bridal headdress.
Turned the other way round, it could be used for the top of a dress or the front of a belt

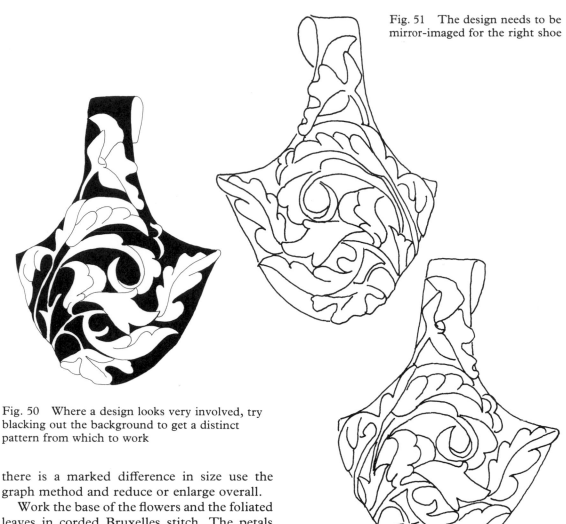

Fig. 51 The design needs to be mirror-imaged for the right shoe

Fig. 50 Where a design looks very involved, try blacking out the background to get a distinct pattern from which to work

there is a marked difference in size use the graph method and reduce or enlarge overall.

Work the base of the flowers and the foliated leaves in corded Bruxelles stitch. The petals and the inside curve of the leaves can be worked in an open-work stitch. This design does not need a great variation of stitches to give it interest, the spaces between the shapes give that anyway, and too many stitches would be confusing.

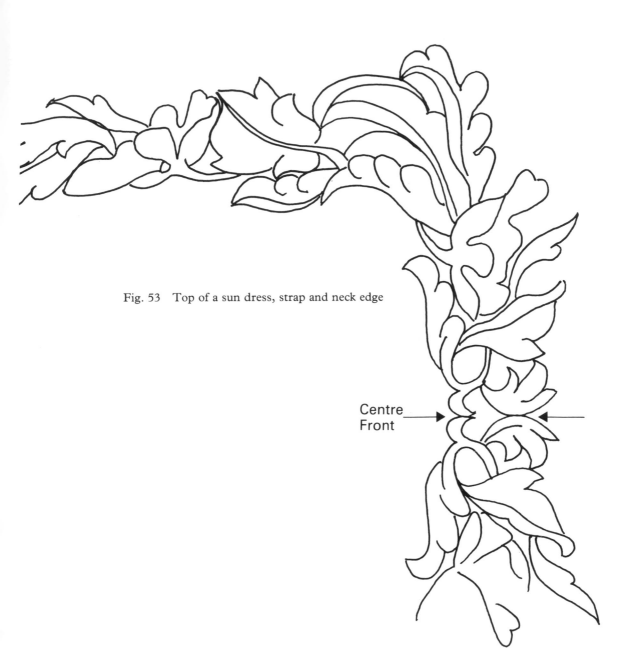

Fig. 53   Top of a sun dress, strap and neck edge

Centre
Front

Fig. 52   Three cap sleeves are needed for each
arm. Make three mirror images for the second
arm. This particular design is best if used for the
left arm; the top flower will then face towards the
front

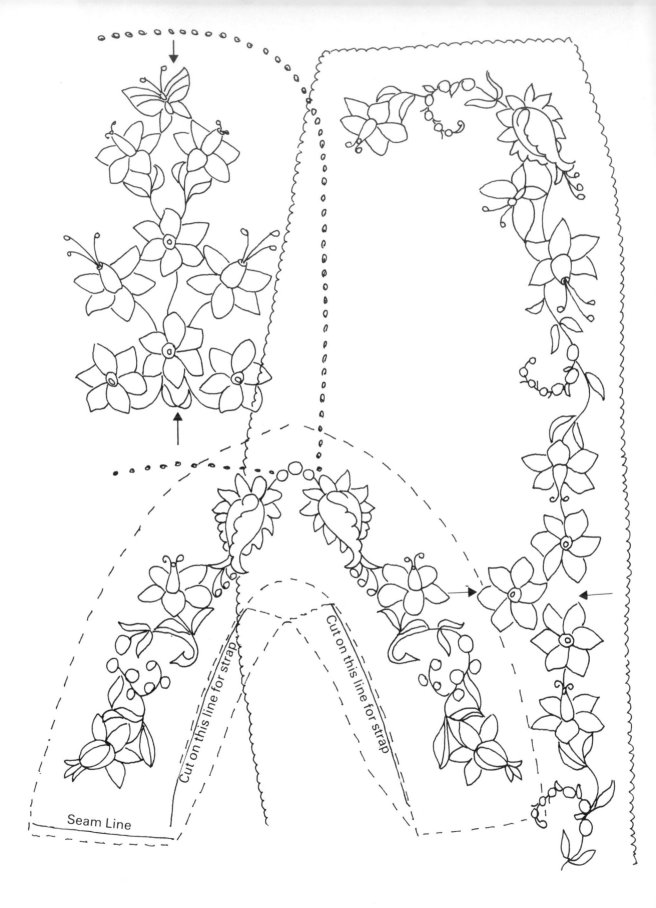

Seam Line

Cut on this line for strap

Cut on this line for strap

THE CHRISTENING SET

These designs are for a bonnet, shoes and a panel that can be used either down the front of a dress or round a small cuff and up the centre of the sleeve.

The bonnet

There are two pieces for the bonnet, the dots show the outline of the back panel, while the wavy line denotes the main front part of the bonnet. Centre top and centre back are marked by the arrows. The two pieces of pattern are cut from the main material used for the christening set, then two pieces are cut from the lining material. Trace the design for the back panel and mark the top and bottom centre points. Mount under film and on to backing material in the usual way.

Work most of the design in corded stitch, highlighting with double and treble Bruxelles

Fig. 54 The dotted line gives part of the back panel of the bonnet; the wavy edge denotes the bonnet front; the arrows indicate the half-way line; the broken line denotes the shoe upper

One of a pair of Christening shoes taken from the design in the book and worked by the author

stitch. The individual motifs are too small to carry any of the other stitches comfortably. The stamens can be embroidered directly on to the material when the lace is transferred. Work the centres of the flowers on the smallest ring of the ring stick which is equivalent to size 11 knitting needle.

Trace off the front panel of the bonnet up to and including the centre flower marked by the arrow. Fold through the centre of this flower and mirror image the other half. Mount and back in the same way as for the shoe and work in the same stitches as those used for the bonnet.

The little scroll of rings and leaves are formed when laying the cordonnet. The rings are then buttonhole stitched all round as the stem is worked. The three centre flowers are worked in the same way as the back panel.

The lace is taken off the backing material, cleaned of couch threads and applied to the bonnet before the lining is attached.

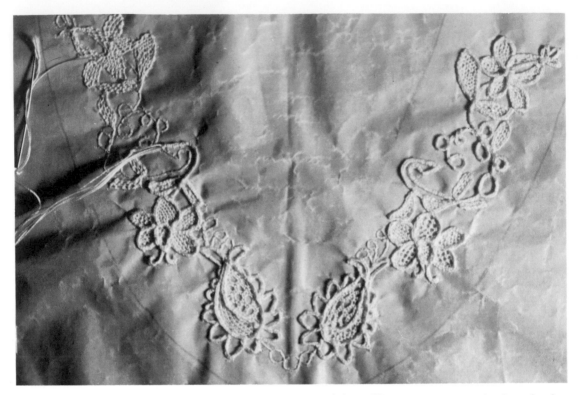

The design being raised

To finish off, work the first edging in this book (*see p. 67*) along the front and round the seam where the back and front panels meet. Ties of ribbon at each end of the panel should be inserted between the material and the lining when they are being sewn together.

The complete design as given for the front of the bonnet can be mirror imaged and used along the front hem of the dress, or can be used as a cuff and up the centre of the sleeve as shown in the small drawing.

The shoe
The shoe pattern is the broken line. To make, cut two uppers of the main material and two linings. Cut two soles allowing for turnings of the main material and two inner soles of the lining without allowing for seams.

Cut two inner soles of interlining (either Vilene or Bonderweb) of the same size. Trace the design, mount and back in the usual way and work in the same stitches as suggested for the bonnet. Remove the lace from the backing

material, pulling out any couch threads that remain. Take an upper of main material, sew the lace into position, using one or two stitches at the tip of each leaf or petal, and catching the rings and stems in place, then embroider the stamens. It is best to work the other shoe as far as this before continuing with the first one.

To make up the shoes, join the heel seams. Make a row of running stitches round the toe of the shoe but do not fasten off. These running stitches are used to draw up to make the upper fit the sole and the exact size will not be known until the soles are in position.

Take the sole cut from the main material, fold in the raw edge and tack down. Fold in the outside edge of the upper and again tack down.

The upper and the sole are now joined together with ladder stitches; these should be invisible when the thread is pulled tight. Ease in the gathers at the toe and, once the two parts are joined, pull the running stitches out. Do the same with one upper and one sole of the lining, adding the interlining to the sole.

When finished, turn the lining inside out and place inside the main shoe, this covers all

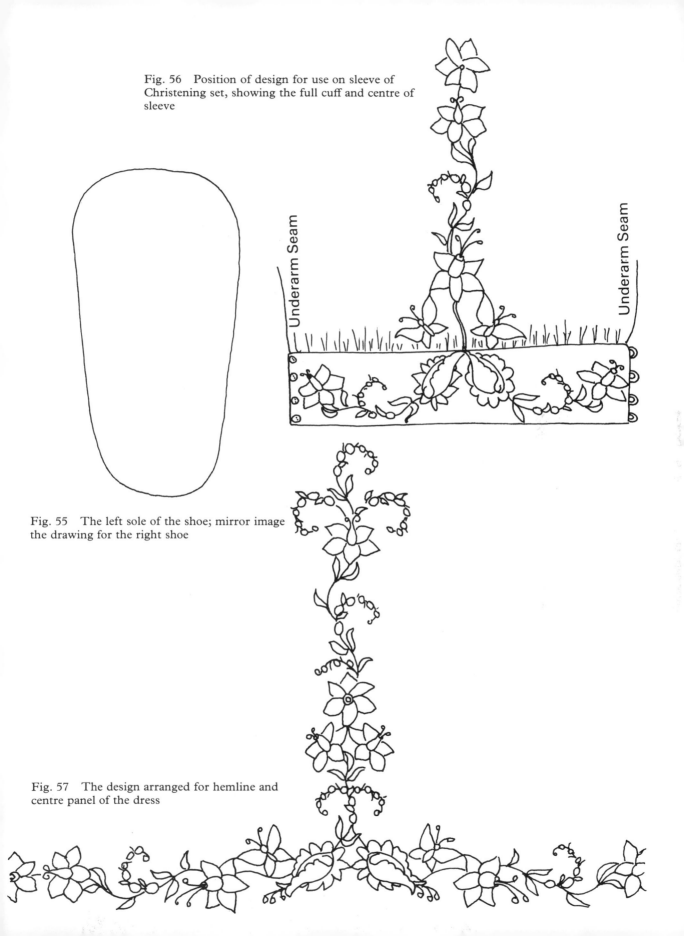

Fig. 56   Position of design for use on sleeve of
Christening set, showing the full cuff and centre of
sleeve

Underarm Seam

Underarm Seam

Fig. 55   The left sole of the shoe; mirror image
the drawing for the right shoe

Fig. 57   The design arranged for hemline and
centre panel of the dress

A miniature version of the parasol

raw seams. Turn in the top edge of the shoe and ladder stitch the main material to the lining. Add ribbons at the heel to tie round the ankle.

The dress panel
The drawing of the sleeve and the hem of the dress shows the position of the lace panel. If the whole design is drawn up to scale this will look just as effective on a toddler's dress.

PARASOLS

Antique parasols are frequently offered for sale with the lace either torn or badly worn, much of it being the early machine lace. If it is handmade then the original lace is worth restoring otherwise it is quicker to make a new cover. Newnham Lace Equipment make replica frames, full size and miniature one-third size for the dolls shown on p. 117.

Preparing the pattern
Parasols usually have eight spines to hold the cover in place and this is where the instructions on p. 58 can be put to practical use. The design given here is based on the principles of Figs 29, 30 and 31. After folding the paper pattern into the eight sections, instead of cutting the top curve into a concave, cut the edge convex, this will give eight points. When the cover is cut to the paper pattern the points of the material are fixed to the ends of the spines. It is intended that the design given for the one-third size parasol should be appliquéd to fine silk net and the work kept light and open to allow for the closing of the frame. For this reason lay the centre motif directly on to the net as a cordon-net and hold it in position by a row of spaced buttonhole stitches. Allow an opening at the centre big enough for the ferrel of the frame to pass through; this can be closed with a short length of edging worked as a ring, placed in position and drawn up after the rest of the work is completed. The first or second edging (*see pp. 67–68*) would be suitable.

The circle of flowers and leaves should be traced off and mounted on to backing material in the usual way. Use two sizes of thread – 130/3s and 100/3s are right for the small parasol; if the design is enlarged up to full size use the

Fig. 58   A design for a miniature parasol cover.
The finished article has small beads sewn to the
ends of the spines

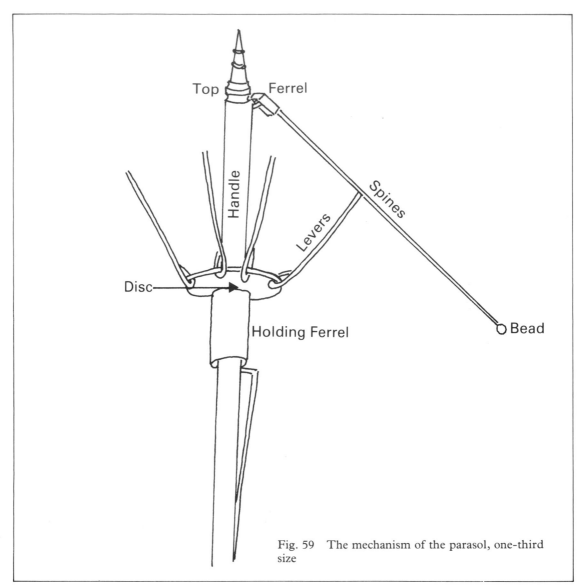

Fig. 59   The mechanism of the parasol, one-third size

equivalent of 60 and 80 crochet cotton. The lining has to be made up of eight sections, all of which can be joined together before fixing inside the frame; the last seam which joins all sections into a circle has to be done once the lining is inside the frame. Close the circle at the top by sewing to the disc that holds the eight spines at the top, then sew the points to the end of the spines (*see Fig. 58*).

Working instructions

The lace can be worked in the following way. Where the leaves appear to curl over, work in corded stitch using the thickest thread. Then, still in corded stitch, work to the centre of each leaf in fine thread; then work a row of veins. Change to the thick thread and work the rest of the leaf in Bruxelles stitch. The stalks are formed by working two rows of Bruxelles stitch in the thick thread; the stems of the flowers and buds are worked the same way, but in the fine thread. The buds can be worked in corded stitch, using the thick thread for the petals and the fine thread for the seedpod. Work the largest of the two hanging petals of the flowers in the second variation of the pea stitch and the smaller petal in double Bruxelles stitch. The turned up sepals of the calyx should be worked in fine thread in Bruxelles stitch. The large sepal is worked in thick thread, the small one at the top in fine thread.

Once the lace has been worked, finish off by working a very fine cordonette held by spaced buttonhole stitches. In no way must the edges be raised unduly or the net will be too stiff to close the frame once the lace has been applied.

If the design is being worked solely as a piece of lace for a centre piece, then all of the edges can be raised to give a sculptured effect. This is best done after the lace has been applied to the background net. The completed mat should then be stitched to a background material to hold it firmly in place to do the raising. In this way the risk of edges curling out of shape is minimised. The net can then be cut close to the edge of the lace, or a cordonnette can be laid round the circumference and raised. The ridge of the buttonhole stitches must lie close to the outside cutting edge.

7.

Poupée and Pandore

This chapter will be of interest to the many doll collectors and those working on the conservation of dolls' clothes. The less experienced lacemaker will find that a doll provides an ideal model on which to try out the newly learnt stitches and design techniques; the collar and parts of patterns of the previous chapter were drawn to scale for a 60 cm (24 in) doll, but can easily be enlarged by the method shown on pp. 80–81.

The first fashion dolls were called *poupées* or *pandores*: *poupées* if the height was over 76·2 cm (2 ft 6 in) and they were dressed for the Court, or *la petite pandore* when a smaller doll was used by the dressmaker to show the morning *déshabille* (the less ornate garments fashionable for morning or afternoon wear). As long ago as 1391 it is known that a certain M. Ladroise of Paris sent a fashion doll to the Queen of England and it is known that the manufacture of dolls was well established by the time Louis XIII was a child as there is a record of him being presented with a little carriage full of them. The *poupée* was in favour as the fashion model for over 500 years, then the dolls were replaced by the fashion plates and these were closely followed by the fashion magazines. The *poupée* was at its height of popularity during the reign of Louis XIV. They were exhibited in the salons of the Hotel Rambouillet with one famous doll being known as *La Grande Pandore*. Together with a smaller version, she was left on exhibition throughout the duration of that particular fashion. These dolls were dressed in all the costly laces, exact in every detail, as were the handmade clothes they displayed.

Another famous *poupée* was shown at the annual fair in Venice, held in the Piazza of St Mark on Ascension Day. After the fair the doll was left on show in a shop on the Pente dei Bareteri for the remainder of the year, allowing the local fashion houses to copy the fine detail. This doll, called *La Poupa di Franza* was well known until the beginning of this century. So, the fashion doll in all its lace and finery has been with us for a long time.

To spend a lot of time dressing a plastic doll would be profane and, in any case, they are poor imitations of their predecessors because they are too tall for the rest of their proportions to allow the clothes of the sixteenth to the nineteenth centuries to lay right. A porcelain doll kit could become an heirloom worth many times its original cost if dressed in detail and with the handmade lace of the period. Instead of providing the fashions of the future, they would give the lacemaker the chance to create the styles that now form part of our history.

The addresses are given (*see p. 117*) of suppliers of doll kits ranging from a 22·86 cm (9 in) to 53·34 cm (21 in). The big one is ideal for getting a lot of detail into the clothes. Figs 97 and 98 show a pattern for the body which will give a good base on which to display the clothes. The dolls used as models in the following photographs were made from the kits mentioned and were made up in the following way.

TO MAKE THE DOLL

First make a tracing of the pattern for the body and enlarge or reduce the design following the instructions on p. 80. Coat the inside of the material with melted soap; this stops the sawdust filling from seeping through.

A Moores doll kit made up and dressed in a costume of the late eighteenth century *c.* 1780. The Lady Pandora is approximately 50 cm (20 in) in height

Balance line from point of neck to foot supporting the weight of the body

Fig. 60   Poupée, period 1870. An added bustle would make the dresses sit correctly

Fig. 61   Fill china legs with cotton wool or foam filling. Join to end of each leg. Place row of stitches through front and back of leg at arrows to allow the doll to sit

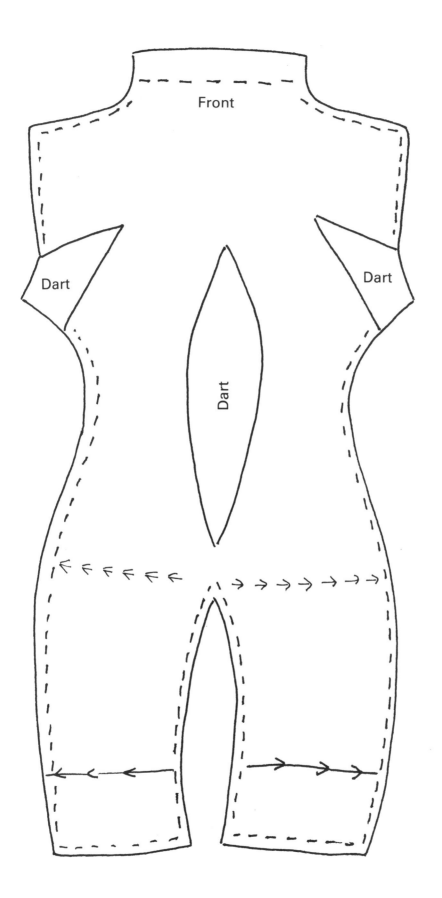

Front

Dart

Dart

Dart

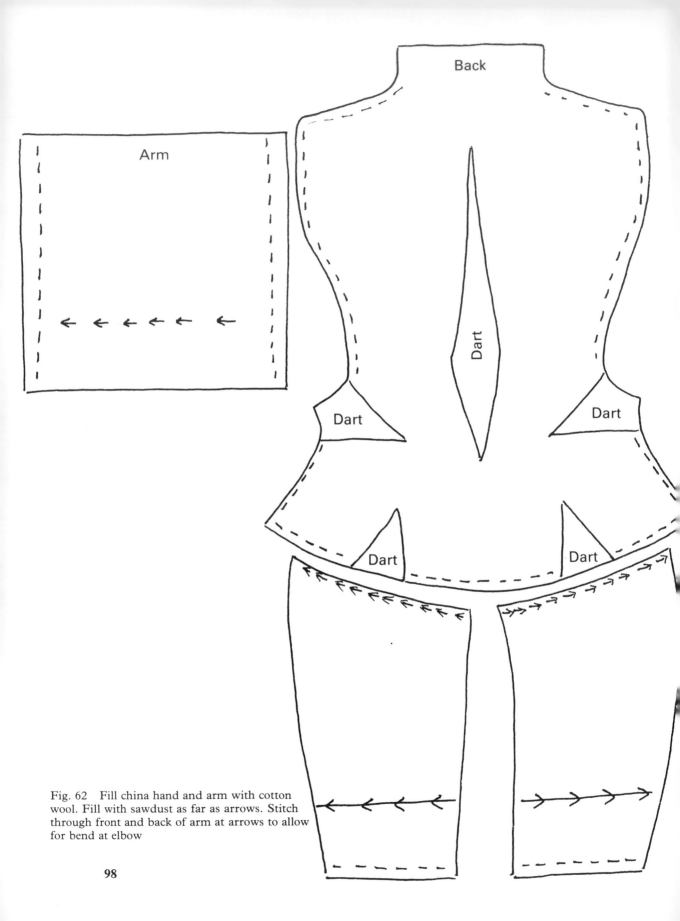

Arm

Back

Dart

Dart

Dart

Dart

Dart

Fig. 62   Fill china hand and arm with cotton wool. Fill with sawdust as far as arrows. Stitch through front and back of arm at arrows to allow for bend at elbow

98

Cut out the pattern for the front, marking the darts, then the back, the two legs and the two arms. Sew all darts before joining anything together. Sew the two back leg pieces to the bottom of the back, then sew back and front of body together down each side from underarm to end of legs. Double stitch all seams. Sew the two arms down the dotted line, forming two tubes. Around the base of each tube work a row of running stitches, using strong buttonhole thread; draw up but do not fasten off. Place a china arm inside the tube, arm first, then draw the running stitches up tight round the groove in the arm. Sew strongly into position and turn the material to the outside. Fill the china arm with foam filling, then loosely fill the material with sawdust as far as the arrows. Backstitch across where marked; this allows the arm to bend. Fill the rest of the arm with sawdust, close the top by turning in the raw edge and oversewing. Make the other arm in the same way.

Sew the inside seams of the legs from the end up to the first set of arrows and fasten off securely. This forms enough tube to insert the legs. Place a row of running stitches round the bottom of each leg. Push the china leg knee first into the tube and fasten off in the same way as the arm pieces. Pull the legs through the top of the body and continue to pull the rest of the body through to turn the material the right side out. Through the opening at the inside top of the legs, first fill the china with foam filling and then turn in the raw edges and oversew each leg up to the join at the body. Fill the legs with sawdust up to the first set of arrows, then backstitch across to allow the legs to bend. Continue to fill the legs to the second set of arrows and backstitch across to allow the doll to sit.

Turn in the raw edges at each shoulder and oversew leaving enough room at the top for the neck of the doll to go through. Continue to fill the body with sawdust as far as the waist. Take a tube from the inside of a roll of polythene wrap, or something similar. (One of the dolls shown has a handful of drinking straws stuck together with adhesive tape and used instead of a cardboard tube because there was not one available at the time.) Push one end into the head and fill the space left with foam filling; place the other end of the tube through the neckline of the material and bed down well into the sawdust at the base of the body. Turn the raw edges in round the top of neck. Then, with a curved needle place a row of running stitches round the top of the material and draw up tightly. Double stitch round the neck before fastening off securely.

Continue to fill the body through the arm openings making sure that the buttocks and the bustline are well defined. Ladies had more flesh on them in those days as it was a reflection on the husbands' financial status.

Close the arm openings by turning in the raw edges and over-sewing back and front sides together. The arms are best just sewn to the body round the top of the shoulder and a little way down the back and the front of the arm opening. This allows the garments to sit better.

A second body pattern was then cut from old kid gloves; the ones used came from a charity shop for a few pence each. The large doll needed four gloves to produce enough kid. The side seams of the gloves were cut and the kid laid flat before pinning on the pattern. Use the part of the glove from the thumb insert up to the top of the glove. The longer the glove, the easier it is to cut out the pattern. DMC cream linen lace thread, size 25, was used to ladder stitch the kid round the ready-made body. No stitches are needed where indicated by the arrows on the pattern because the kid is so supple that it follows the lines of the material body easily.

DRESSING THE DOLL

When dressing the doll it will be necessary to make a separate bustle to set the clothes off. The first small edgings in the book would be ideal for undergarments, giving the reader a chance to work with fine threads without undertaking a large scale project. Basic changes in fashion were slow to materialise, and the same undergarments can be used over a long span of time. After 1820 drawers became part of a woman's undergarments. These were just two long tight-fitting tubes on a waistband with a drawstring of braid. The bottom of the legs had lace frills, sometimes reaching as far as the knees.

The seventeenth century

Petticoats often had large tucks around the hips to give fullness to the dresses. From the beginning of the seventeenth century the embroidered and lace-edged hoop petticoats, along with the busk of wood called the stomacher, was worn and continued to be so for nearly 80 years. There was a top dress of heavier material over an underdress. The overskirt opened down the front and the sleeves of the top bodice were slashed to show the lace sleeves of the underbodice. The underskirt was often of tiers of lace one on top of the other or made up of flounces, one gathered and joined to the next. The tops, which were known as 'boddies' of both under- and overdresses were separate from the skirts and held together with tapes. Special pins for this purpose had a fitted cap that was pushed hard down on to the point. This stopped the wearer from being scratched. The tapes were called 'Lacis' and were made on a lycet, giving a very strong four-sided braid. This type of braid was used for drawing together the bodices of the top garment and for holding up the petticoats. Among the garments made with lace over the period were the fichu, the ruff and the falling collar.

Shoes were trimmed with lace, often in the form of a large rose on the instep, and lace would be sewn round the top edges of shoes and boots. During this period shoes and boots had thick high heels and were made of rich brocade.

The pompadour, a high, wire frame, lavish with lace of the Venetian type, was worn on the head. The Venetian lace was followed by the softer laces along with masses of ribbons as the pompadour grew higher.

Hanging pockets were tied round the waist with tapes and were reached through an opening left in both gown and petticoat. Lace edged the lawn handkerchiefs that were used by men and women, much bigger than the ones used now, some as much as 76·2 cm (2 ft 6 in) square; there was often only a very small square of lawn, the rest was lace.

Towards the later part of the seventeenth century, jacket bodices were worn for 'Undress Wear', a contempary term used to describe clothes that were shorter than the full dress worn on formal occasions.

The eighteenth century

At the beginning of the eighteenth century loose fitting and flowing dresses, some with pleats falling from the neckline, became popular. Lace at this period was being worn with everything: elbow-length sleeves had falling cuffs of lace to the wrists and the chemise was part of everyday wear. Large triangles of lace were worn for evening wear and fine poplin or muslin with lace insertions or edgings was used through the day. For a while lace caps were also worn during the day, some were just triangles with long side pieces called lappets. Large collars, called pelerines, also had long lappets that were tucked into a belt at the waist. Aprons were worn by small boys, girls of all ages and women. The children's aprons were full length in front and came down to the waist at the back, with either full sleeves or very wide frills and were called 'pin-afores' because they were pinned to the front of their everyday clothes. These tops when used in the afternoon had as much expensive lace on them as the dresses they were supposed to keep clean.

The nineteenth century

In the nineteenth century the waistline was higher, sleeves were tight, skirts were ankle length, deep lace flounces fell from the waist to hem, deep-berthe collars and lace-trimmed poke bonnets, were popular, as were small straw hats, or pill box hats, with lace veils hanging from the back. These small hats were always perched high on the hair at such an angle it was a wonder they ever stayed on. By the mid-nineteenth century bustles were fashionable, the high-boned collar and blouses with fronts of lace were called plastrons; modesty vests and chemises of lace were to be seen on all the best-dressed ladies. In fact, lace was worn by one and all, because the machine and chemical lace had flooded the market.

Overall design of the lappets

Fig. 63 Styles of headdress predominent between 1860 and 1870

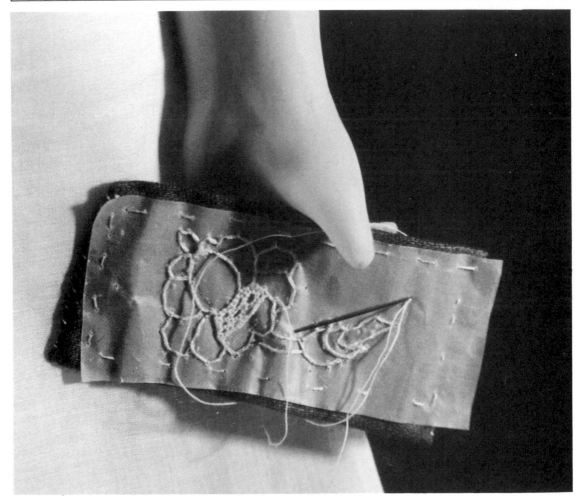

Close-up of the needlepoint lace work being held in the doll's hand

A Moore Dolls' kit of a 'Young Gel' – front view

'Young Gel' back view

Detail of the reticule held by the
Lady Pandora

A Riddingscraft doll kit, made up and getting
ready for Ascot

Detail of a part of a plastron being worked by Kay
(Supersonic) Anderson – again a first piece

The twentieth century

Real lace was very much in evidence right through to the 1920s and, at a price, could still be bought until the Second World War, which means that any pre-war doll could be dressed as a 'flapper' of the 'twenties, for lace trimmed most items of clothing then. Whole evening dresses were made of it, including long trains, and underwear and nightwear were excessively trimmed. Large picture hats were held in place with long lace scarves and everyone had a garter trimmed with lace; even dolls that were sold at that time came complete with garter!

A final point of interest is that until 1675 men had the monopoly of making all clothes, for men and women. They were the tailors and had their own Guild. It was Louis XIV who gave women the right to make clothes for their own sex, giving them the title of couturiers with the right to their own Guild. Even then they were allowed to make only certain garments and any boy over the age of eight was dressed by a tailor. Lacemakers worked to all the Ell measurements, which differed in England, Scotland and the Continent. The English yard has been the standard measure since Henry I decreed that a yard should be the length of his arm. There had been so many confusing ways of measuring until then; the thumb measure was the biggest hoax. From the middle knuckle of the thumb up to the top was called an inch. The person with the largest thumb was always to hand to measure the goods which were being brought into stock, while the lady with the smallest thumb measured the material on its way back across the counter to the customer. One way of paying for lace was to cover it with shilling pieces, the size of the present 5p; the number of coins it took to cover the piece was the price paid to the worker.

Any reader interested in dressing a *poupée* or *pandore* should decide on the period that appeals to her most, and stay with the clothes of that time; the doll collector with an old doll to restore should find the date of the doll and keep the period.

Conclusion

The stitches and working methods covered in this book are the simplest and most common examples of needlepoint lace, but you will find that there is plenty of material to produce effective and attractive results. The photographs, except where they feature antique lace, are all projects worked by relatively inexperienced students – in some cases, indeed, they are their first pieces. This book is intended as an introduction and, once you have mastered the basic principles, you will find it easy to progress to the more intricate stitch patterns and designs. *The Technique of Needlepoint Lace* examines the various types of traditional needlepoint lace in detail and gives working instructions for the different grounds and fillings, some of which are mentioned in passing in this present volume. *Creative Designs in Needlepoint Lace* examines the possibilities for needlepoint lace today and gives ideas for modern interpretations of the traditional motifs. The following photographs show ways in which students have developed their basic skills; perhaps their ideas will prompt you to start experimenting yourself.

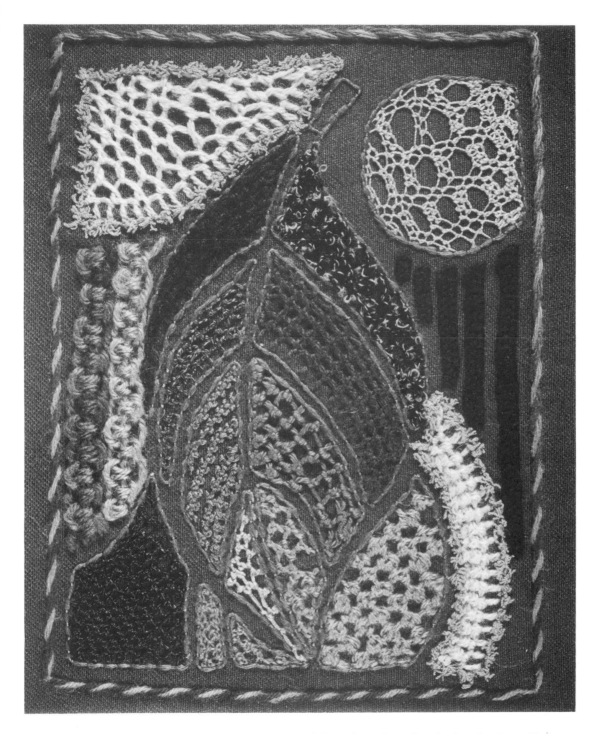

A first piece of needlepoint lace by Anne Forbes-Cockell, in wools and textured threads, to encourage those who don't feel they can cope with fine work

Needlepoint lace stitches can be used in
conjunction with embroidery in many different
ways. This garden gate scene is worked in silks of
spring colours by the author

Conventional lace and experimental work can go
together as has been proved by Pat Gibson
here – she has used an airfix model as a template.
This blue-tit is life-size and is worked in 130/3
and 100/3 coloured silks

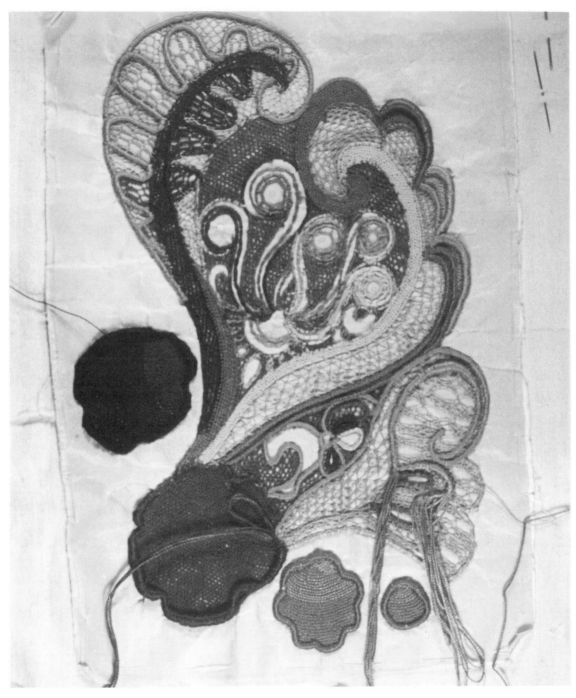

Needlepoint lace has its place in modern fashion.
It can be used to make sophisticated evening wear;
this design for a zouave (a bolero-type jacket
popular in the 1860s) was worked by Shirley
Warren in jewel colours. The design is featured in
Creative Design in Needlepoint Lace

112

Another way to experiment with needlepoint lace is to create free-standing designs. Free-standing lace flowers are reasonably quick to work because each individual flower is small and worked in straightforward stitches. These anemones, by Doreen Holmes, are worked in brilliant coloured 100/3s silks and displayed on natural wood. Further ideas for lace bouquets will be found in *Creative Design in Needlepoint Lace*

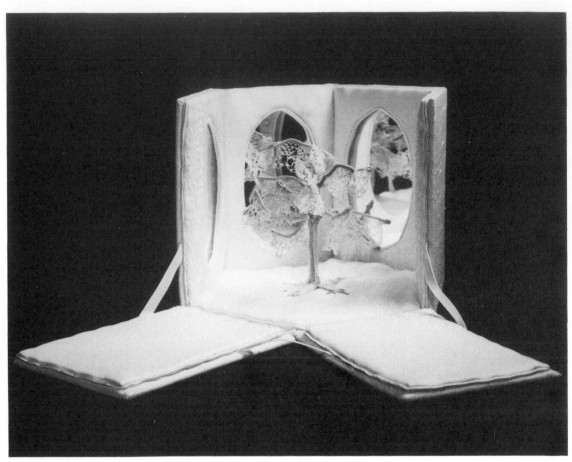

A free-standing tree in a silk-lined and
embroidered, hexagonal-shaped box; worked by
Mary Anderson and exhibited in Japan.
(*Photograph courtesy of Malcolm Powell*)

A close-up of the tree. (*Photograph courtesy of
Malcolm Powell*)

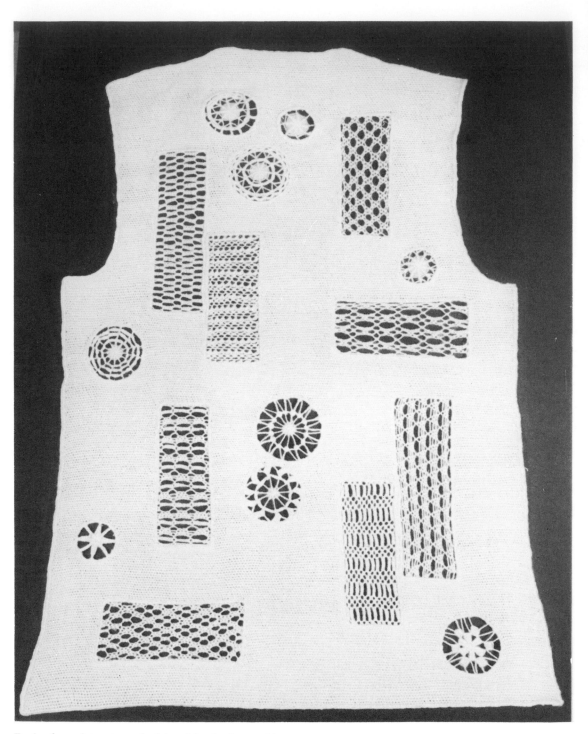

Back of a waistcoat, worked in white 1-ply wool by
Doreen Holmes. The geometric designs and
wheels are all featured in *Creative Design in
Needlepoint Lace*

Suppliers

UNITED KINGDOM

D J Hornsby
149 High Street
Burton Latimer
Kettering
Northamptonshire
Threads, needles, pins, etc.

Mr A Sells
49 Pedley Lane
Clifton
Shefford
Bedfordshire
Threads, pins, needles, etc.

Ken & Pat Schultz
Ixworth Road
Honington
Nr Bury St Edmunds
Suffolk
Books, pillows and carrying cases

Leonie Cox
The Old School
Childswickham
Near Broadway
Worcestershire WR12 7HD
Pure silks

Jack Piper
Silverdale
Flax Lane
Glemsford
Suffolk CO10 7RS
Pure silks

The English Lace School
Honiton Court
Rockbeare
Near Exeter
Devon EX5 2EF
Books, threads, needles and pins

Mace & Nairn
89 Crane Street
Salisbury
Wiltshire
Books, needles, thread, etc.

T Brown
Woodside
Greenlands Lane
Prestwood
Great Missenden
HP16 0QY
Ring sticks

G Hall
90 Shrewsbury Crescent
Humbledon
Sunderland
Tyne and Wear SR3 4AR
Afficots, ring boxes and other fine tools

Newnham Lace Equipment
15 Marlow Close
Basingstoke
Hants RG24 9DD
Pillows and stands

Deighton Brothers Ltd
Riverside Road
Barnstable
North Devon EX31 1LS
Transfers

Busy Hands Crafts
5/7 Denmark Street
Wokingham
Berks RG11 2AY
Beginners' kits

Recollect Doll Supplies
83a Trafalgar Street
Brighton
East Sussex BN1 4EB
Doll kits

Ridings Craft
4–6 Brandycarr
Kirkhamgate
Wakefield
Yorkshire WF2 0RG
Doll kits

Moore Dolls
15 Dealne Drive
Winnersh
Berkshire RG11 5AT
Bisque original and reproduction dolls

UNITED STATES

Arachne Web works
1227 S W Morrison
Portland
Oregon 97205
General supplies

Berga-Ullman, Inc
PO Box 918
North Adams
Massachusetts 01247
Materials and equipment

Frederick J Fawcett
129 South Street
Boston
Massachusetts 02130
Large selection of linen yarns and threads

Osma G Tod Studio
319 Mendoza Avenue
Coral Gables
Florida 33134
Books, instructions, materials and equipment

Robin and Russ Handweavers
533 N Adams Street
McMinnville
Oregon 97128
Books, materials and equipment

Some Place
2990 Adeline Street
Berkeley
California 94703
Books, instructions, materials and equipment

The Unique and Art Lace Cleaners
5926 Delmar Boulevard
St Louis
Missouri 63112
Professional lace cleaning and restoration

Serendipity Shop
1547 Ellin wood
Des Plaines
Illinois 60014
General supplies

Lacis
2990 Adeline Street
Berkley
California 94703–2590
Books, threads, needles and pins

Richard Grantlick
5522 Sherrier Place
NW Washington DC 20016
Silk thread

Zabel Arakelian
29884 Muirland Drive
Garmington Hills
Michigan 48018
Custom-made pillows

Robbins Bobbins
Rte 1 Box 294–1
Mineral Bluff
Georgia 30559
Custom-made pillows, linen, books

Index

Acetate film   24, 25
Afficot   7
Alençon
   bars   44
   beads   44

Backing material   25
Bars or brides   7, 12, 42
   Raleigh   43
Bruxelles stitch   11
Burano lace   15
Buttonhole   7
   rings   53
   stitch   7

Casket   7
Collars
   No. 1   74–6
   No. 2   77–9
Coralline Point   15
Corded stitch   34
Cordonnet   7, 25
Cordonnette   7, 11
Couching   7
Couronnes   7, 12, 53, 54

Decreasing   28, 55
Designing   55, 65

Edging   67–73
Ell   7
Engrêlure   7, 19
Enlarging and reducing   80–1

Flat lace   15
Flemish lace stitch   41
Fil de Trace   70
Fillings   30, 40
Foundation threads   11

Grounds   7, 30

Increasing   28

Jewel in the Crown, The
   first veil   frontispiece
   second veil   10

La trace   7

Machine-made tapes   18
Materials   22
Meshwork   12

Needlepoint lace in relation to embroidery   8,
   15, 16, 28, 29, 110, 114
Needles   22

Pandore and poupée   7, 94–108
Patterns   24, 58–65, 67–79, 82–92
Picots   7, 11, 44
   loop   44
   Venetian   45
Pillows   24
Pin stitch   7, 21
Point
   d'Alençon   13
   d'Argentan   13
   de France   13
   de Gaze   13
   de Venise à Réseau   17
Preparation   22, 25
Projects   58–65
Punto
   in Aria   10
   Tagliato   15–16
Purls   7, 45

Raised work   7, 48
Raising   49
Réseau   7
Reticella   10

Ringsticks   7, 53
Ruskin, John   8

Samplers   27
Scallops   12
Spanish lace   13
Stitches
    Church lace   39
    corded Bruxelles   34
    double Bruxelles   31
    pea   36, 37
    Point d'Anvers   39
    single Bruxelles   31
    Spider web filling   40
    treble Bruxelles   31

Tape lace   7, 18, 19, 20
Thimbles   22
Threads   22
Toile   7

Veins   7, 45, 46
Venetian
    Gros Point   12
    Point de Neige   13
    Rose Point   12

Whipped stitch   35
Working to the sections of a circle   58, 65

Youghal lace   17